Spotter's Guide to
TREES

Esmond Harris
Director of the Royal Forestry Society

Illustrated by
Annabel Milne & Peter Stebbing

D1355115

Contents

3 How to Use this Book
4 Parts of a Tree
6 Conifers
24 Broadleaved Trees
49 Shrubs
52 Identifying Winter Buds
54 Bark Quiz
55 Making Bark Rubbings
56 Match the Fruits to the Trees
58 Growing Seedlings
60 Books to Read/ Places to Visit
62 Index
63 Scorecard

Designed by
Sally Burrough

Edited by
Ingrid Selberg and
Sue Jacquemier

Additional illustrations by
Christine Howes

Printed in Great Britain

First published in 1978 by
Usborne Publishing Limited,
Usborne House,
83-85 Saffron Hill, London EC1N 8RT

© 1985, 1978 by Usborne Publishing Limited

All rights reserved. No part of this publication may be reproduced, stored in a retrieval system, or transmitted by any means, electronic, mechanical, photocopying, recording, or otherwise, without the prior permission of the publisher.

Acknowledgements
The illustrators would like to acknowledge the help of the staff of the Royal Botanical Gardens at Kew, with special thanks to Ruth Messom. They also thank Dr Martin Rix at the Royal Horticultural Society Gardens at Wisley, and Peter Orriss of the Cambridge University Botanical Gardens.

The name Usborne and the device are Trade Marks of Usborne Publishing Ltd.

How to Use this Book

This book is an identification guide to some of the trees of Britain and Europe. Take it with you when you go out spotting. Not all of these trees will be common in your area, but many may be found in large gardens or parks. (See page 60 for a list of places to visit.)

The book is arranged with conifers first, followed by broad-leaved trees and shrubs. Trees that are closely related, for example all the Oaks, are grouped together.

The illustrations show important features that will help you to identify a tree at any time of the year. For each type of tree, the leaf, the bark, the shape of a full-grown tree in full leaf and its shape in winter (if the tree is deciduous) are always shown. Flowers and fruits (including cones) are also illustrated if they will help you to identify the tree.

The description next to each illustration gives you additional information to help you identify trees. The average height of a full-grown tree is written next to each illustration.

Remember that there are many clues to help you recognize a tree, not just the leaves, so look carefully at the bark, the tree's shape and other features.

Beside the description is a small blank circle. Each time you spot a new tree, make a tick in the circle.

Scorecard

At the back of the book is a scorecard which gives you a score for each tree you spot. A common tree scores 5 points, and a very rare one is worth 25 points. If you like, you can add up your score after a day out spotting.

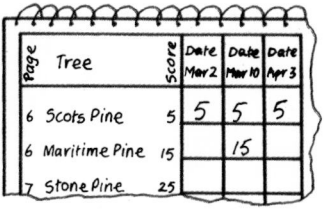

Page	Tree	Score	Date Mar 2	Date Mar 10	Date Apr 3
6	Scots Pine	5	5	5	5
6	Maritime Pine	15		15	
7	Stone Pine	25			

Parts of a Tree

A tree is a plant that grows on a single, central woody stem. A shrub is usually smaller and has many stems.

Trees are divided into two main groups: **conifers** and **broadleaved trees.** Most broadleaved trees have broad flat leaves (which they drop in winter) and they have seeds which are enclosed in fruits (nuts or other forms). Most conifers have narrow, needle-like or scaly leaves. Their fruits are usually woody cones.

Most broadleaved trees are **deciduous** which means that they lose their leaves in the autumn and grow new ones again in the spring. Most conifers are **evergreen,** meaning that they keep their green leaves throughout the winter.

These pictures show the different parts of a tree and explain some of the words that appear in the book.

Leaves

There are many different shapes of leaves. Some of the most common ones are shown here.
A leaf that is in one piece is called **simple.**

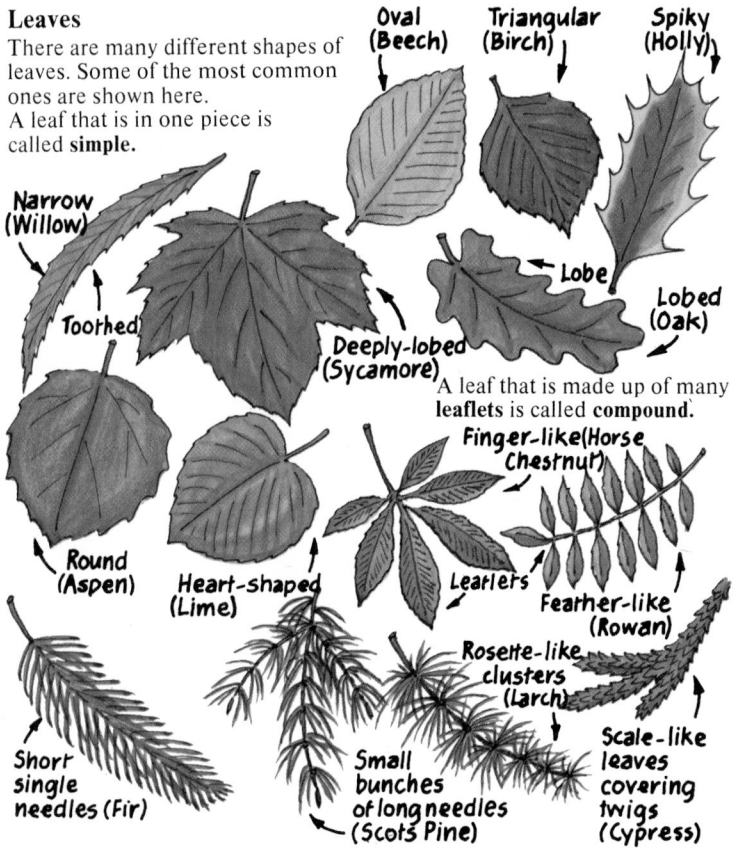

A leaf that is made up of many **leaflets** is called **compound.**

Flowers

All trees have flowers that develop into fruits. Here are some different types of flowers.

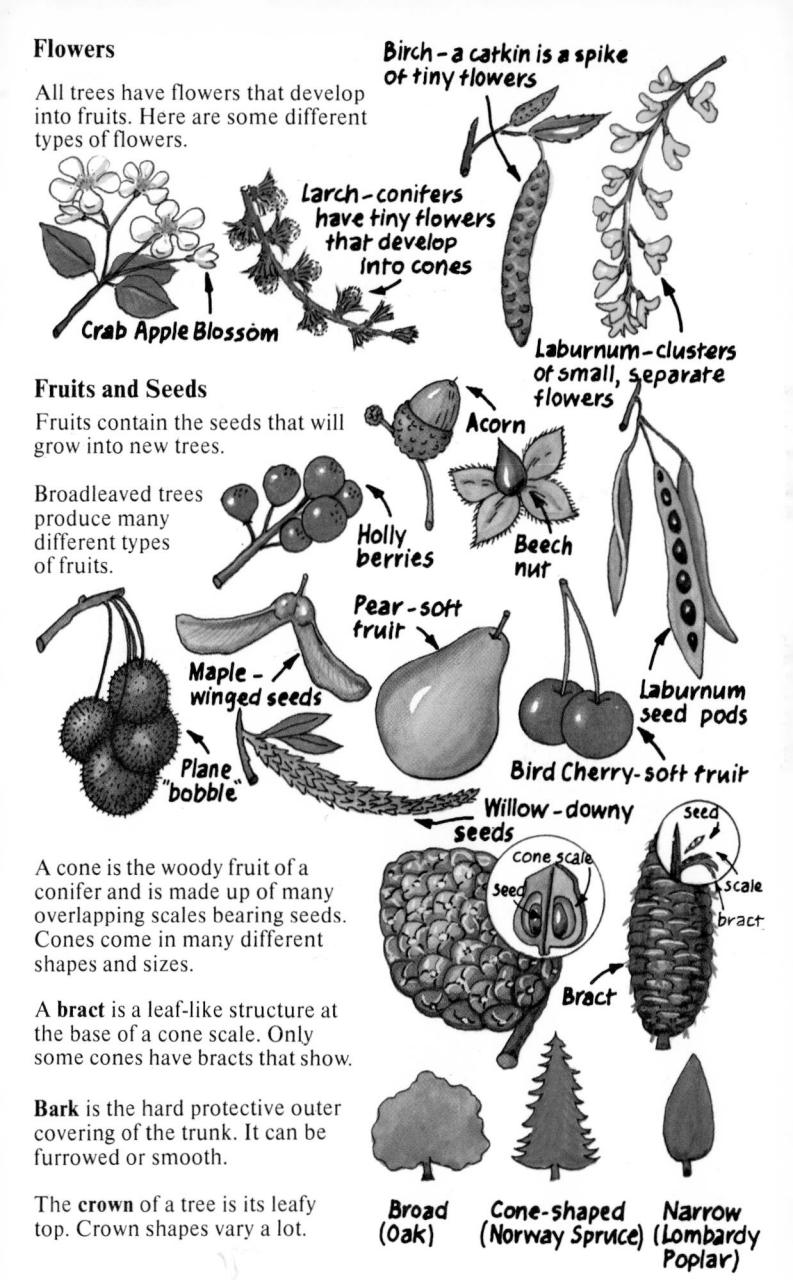

Fruits and Seeds

Fruits contain the seeds that will grow into new trees.

Broadleaved trees produce many different types of fruits.

A cone is the woody fruit of a conifer and is made up of many overlapping scales bearing seeds. Cones come in many different shapes and sizes.

A **bract** is a leaf-like structure at the base of a cone scale. Only some cones have bracts that show.

Bark is the hard protective outer covering of the trunk. It can be furrowed or smooth.

The **crown** of a tree is its leafy top. Crown shapes vary a lot.

Conifers

Small bud

Long, bare trunk is red near top of tree

Short, paired needles

Green, pointed cone turns brown in second year

Bark flakes off in "plates"

▲ Scots Pine

Short, blue-green, paired needles. Small pointed buds. Upper bark red, but grey and furrowed below. Young tree pointed, becoming flat-topped with age.

Long, paired needles

Cones are on tree for several years

Long bud

▲ Maritime Pine

Long, stout, grey-green, paired needles. Long, spindle-shaped buds. Long, shiny brown cones in clusters. Rugged bark on long, bare trunk.

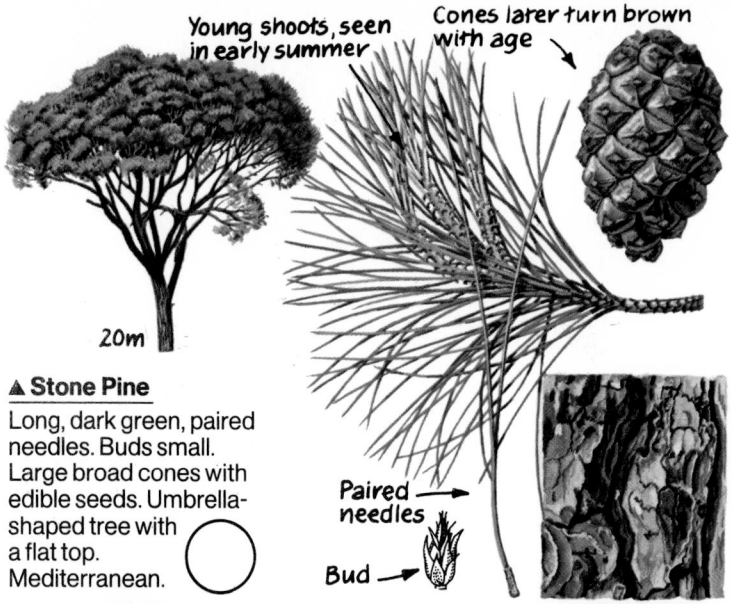

▲ Stone Pine

Long, dark green, paired needles. Buds small. Large broad cones with edible seeds. Umbrella-shaped tree with a flat top. Mediterranean.

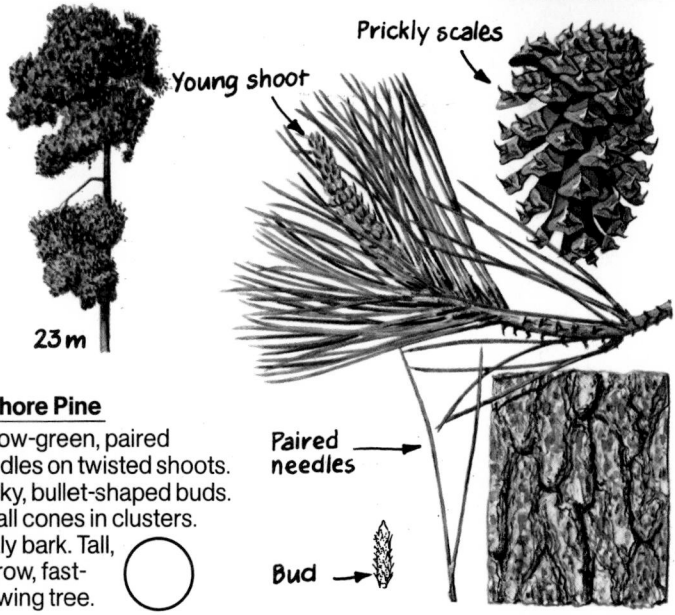

▲ Shore Pine

Yellow-green, paired needles on twisted shoots. Sticky, bullet-shaped buds. Small cones in clusters. Scaly bark. Tall, narrow, fast-growing tree.

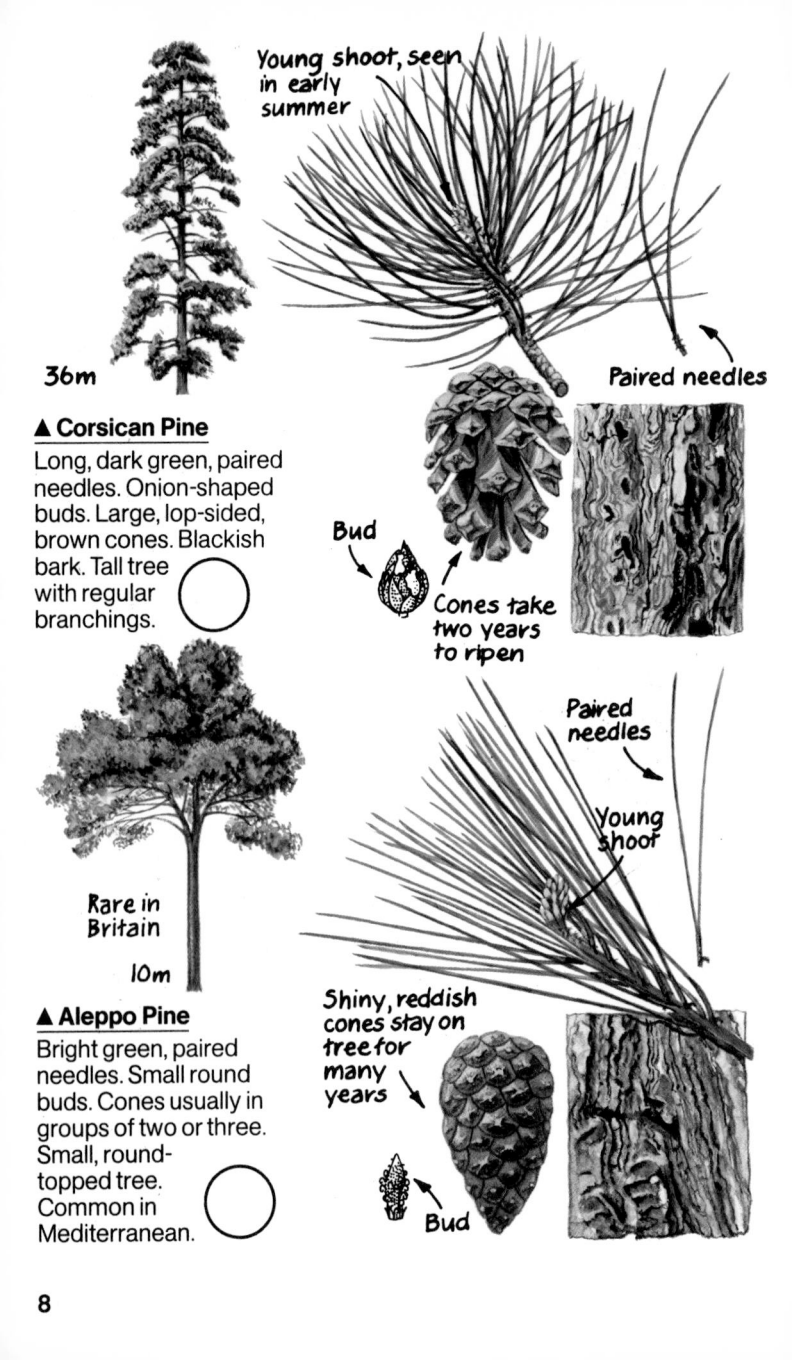

▲ Corsican Pine

Long, dark green, paired needles. Onion-shaped buds. Large, lop-sided, brown cones. Blackish bark. Tall tree with regular branchings.

▲ Aleppo Pine

Bright green, paired needles. Small round buds. Cones usually in groups of two or three. Small, round-topped tree. Common in Mediterranean.

▲ Swiss Stone Pine

Dense, stiff needles in fives. Small, pointed, sticky buds. Egg-shaped cones, with edible seeds, ripen and fall in third year. Cone-shaped tree.

▲ Monterey Pine

Slender, grass green needles in threes. Large, pointed, sticky buds. Cones squat, growing flat against branches, staying on tree for many years.

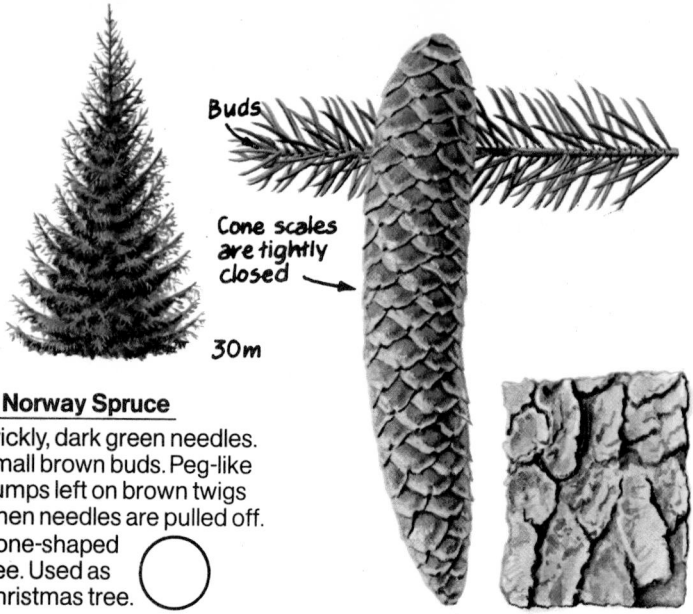

▲ Norway Spruce

Prickly, dark green needles. Small brown buds. Peg-like bumps left on brown twigs when needles are pulled off. Cone-shaped tree. Used as Christmas tree.

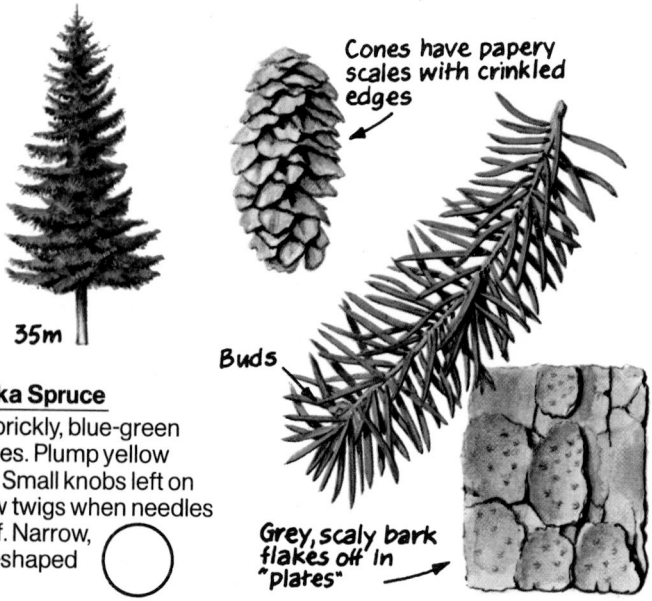

▲ Sitka Spruce

Very prickly, blue-green needles. Plump yellow buds. Small knobs left on yellow twigs when needles fall off. Narrow, cone-shaped trees.

▲ European Larch

Bunches of soft, light green needles, which fall in winter, leaving small knobs on twigs. Female flowers are reddish. Small egg-shaped cones.

▲ Japanese Larch

Bunches of blue-green needles, falling in winter. Orange twigs. Female flowers are pinkish-green. Small, rosette-like cones.

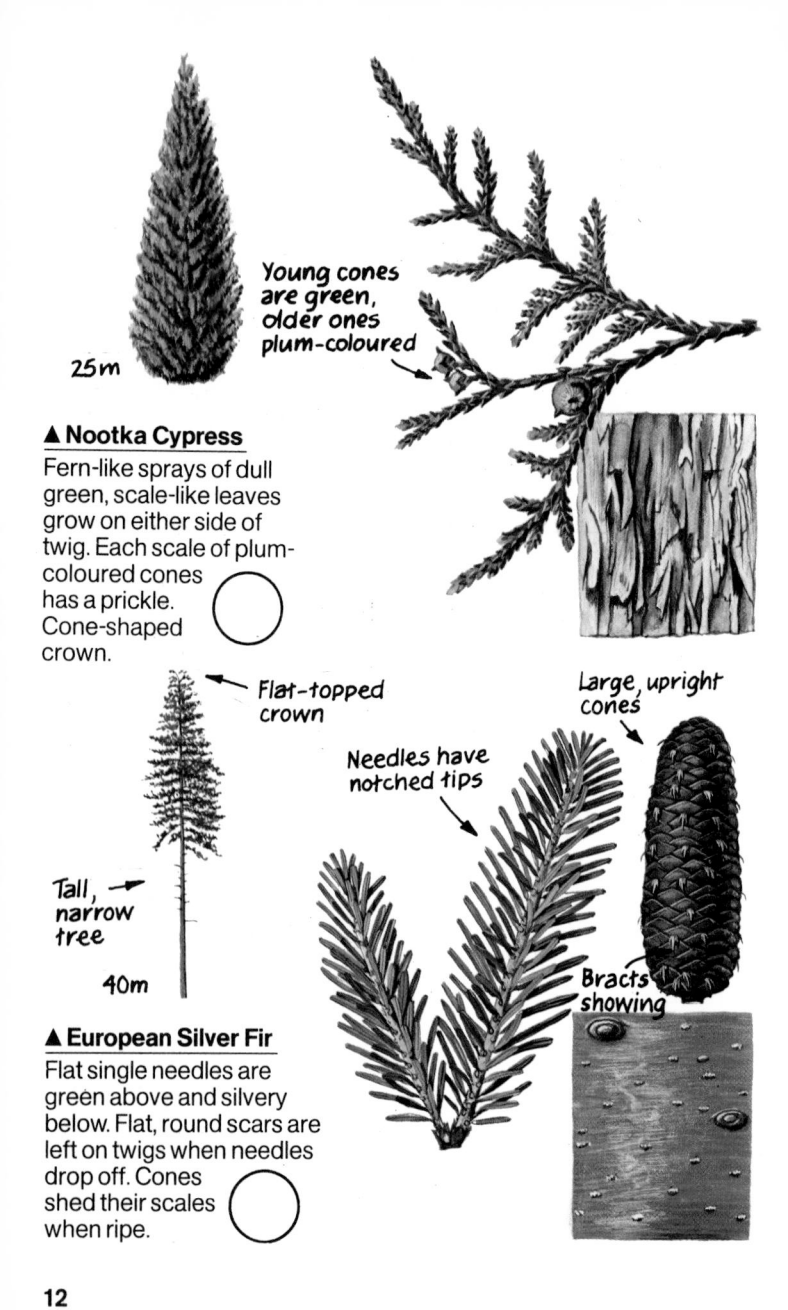

▲ Nootka Cypress

Fern-like sprays of dull green, scale-like leaves grow on either side of twig. Each scale of plum-coloured cones has a prickle. Cone-shaped crown.

▲ European Silver Fir

Flat single needles are green above and silvery below. Flat, round scars are left on twigs when needles drop off. Cones shed their scales when ripe.

30m

▲ Greek Fir

Shiny green, spiny-tipped needles all round twig. Tall, narrow cones shed scales to leave bare spike on tree. Common in parks.

28m

▲ Spanish Fir

Short, blunt, blue-grey needles all round twig. Cylindrical, upright cones fall apart on tree. Found only in gardens in Britain.

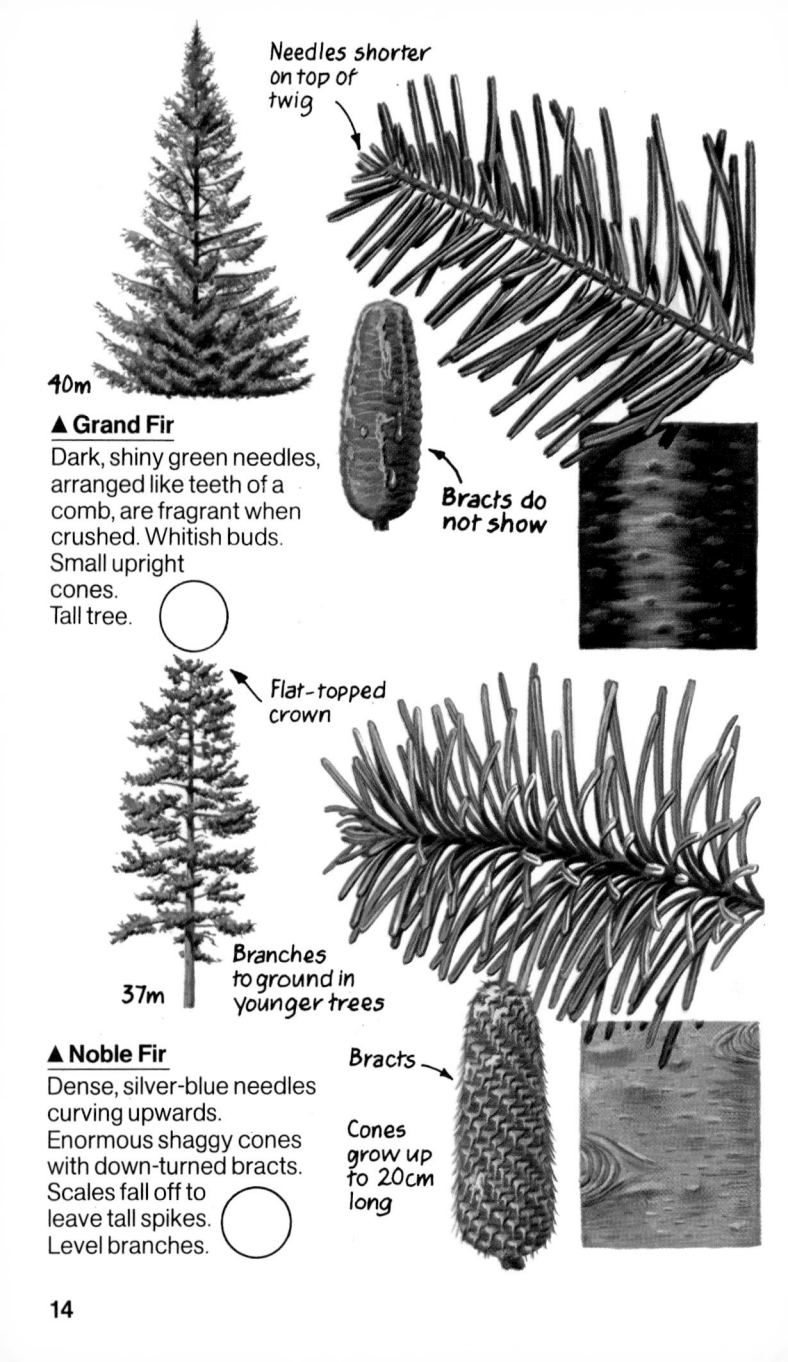

▲ Grand Fir

Dark, shiny green needles, arranged like teeth of a comb, are fragrant when crushed. Whitish buds. Small upright cones. Tall tree.

▲ Noble Fir

Dense, silver-blue needles curving upwards. Enormous shaggy cones with down-turned bracts. Scales fall off to leave tall spikes. Level branches.

▲ Douglas Fir

Soft fragrant needles. Long-pointed, copper-brown buds. Light brown, hanging cones with three-pointed bracts. Old bark is thick and corky.

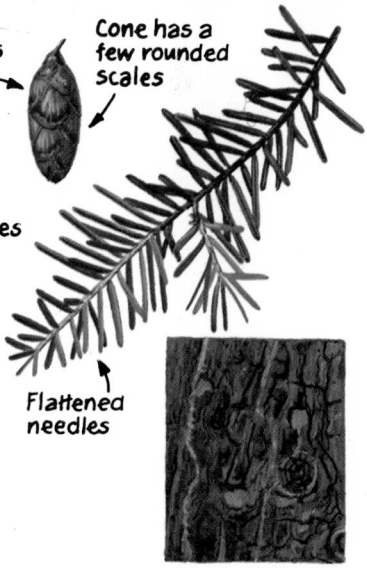

▲ Western Hemlock

Needles various lengths, green above and silver below. Small cones on shoot tips. Smooth, brown scaly bark. Branch tips and top shoot droops.

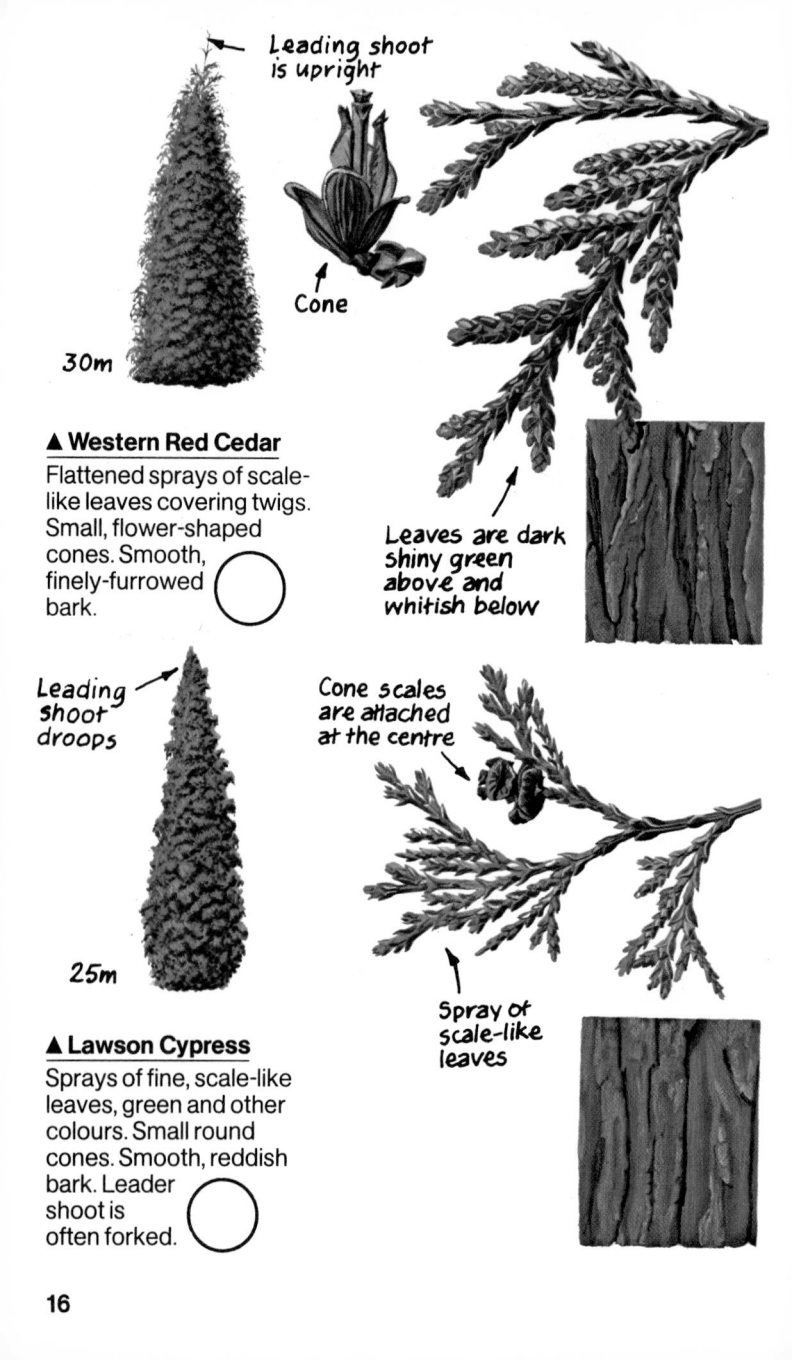

▲ Western Red Cedar

Flattened sprays of scale-like leaves covering twigs. Small, flower-shaped cones. Smooth, finely-furrowed bark.

▲ Lawson Cypress

Sprays of fine, scale-like leaves, green and other colours. Small round cones. Smooth, reddish bark. Leader shoot is often forked.

15m

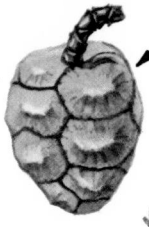

Cones are shiny pale green at first, dull grey when older

Leaves are smaller than those of Monterey Cypress

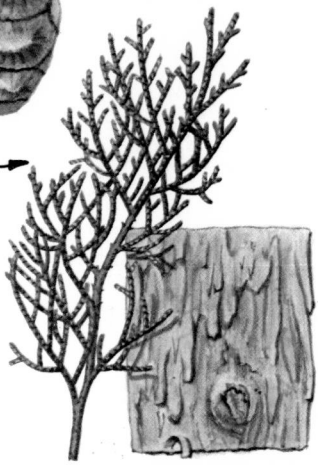

▲ Italian Cypress

Small, dark, dull-green, scale-like leaves, closely pressed to stem. Large, grey, rounded cones. An upright, narrow-crowned tree. Mainly ornamental.

25m

Leaves are lemon-scented when crushed

Knob

Peeling bark

▲ Monterey Cypress

Dense sprays of small, scale-like leaves. Large, purplish-brown, rounded cones with knob on scales. Column-shaped when young, flat-topped when old.

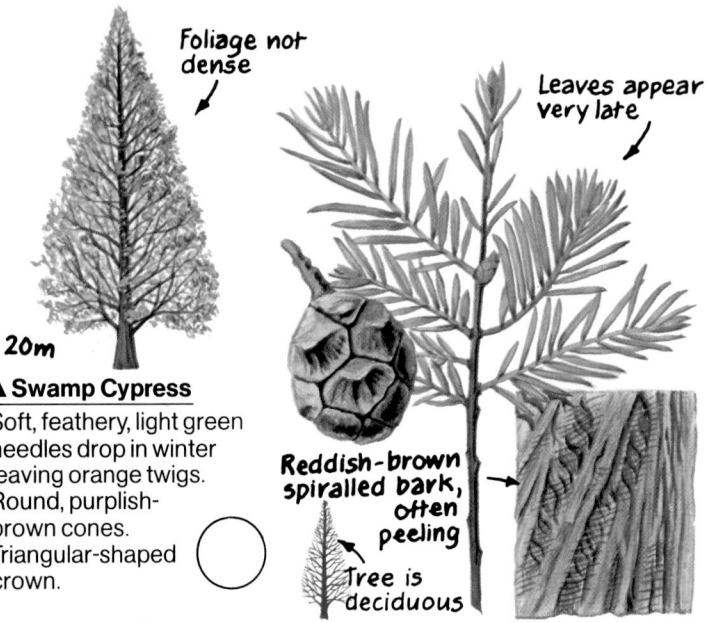

▲ Swamp Cypress

Soft, feathery, light green needles drop in winter leaving orange twigs. Round, purplish-brown cones. Triangular-shaped crown.

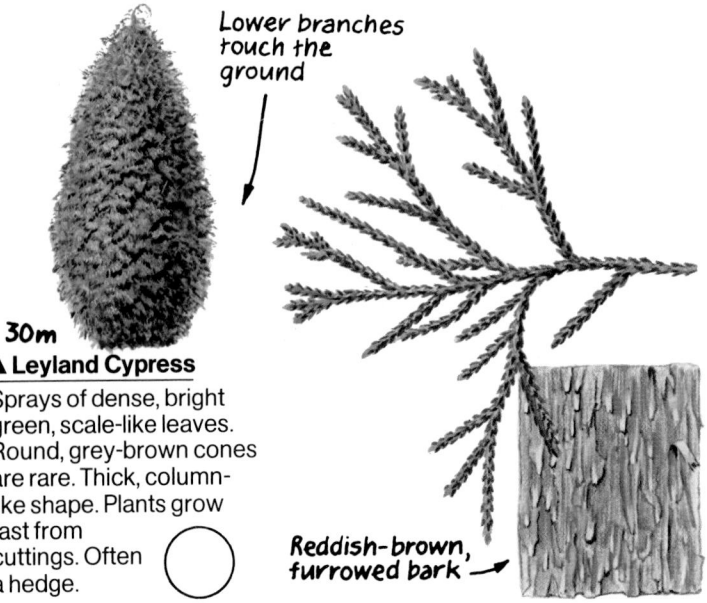

▲ Leyland Cypress

Sprays of dense, bright green, scale-like leaves. Round, grey-brown cones are rare. Thick, column-like shape. Plants grow fast from cuttings. Often a hedge.

▲ Japanese Red Cedar

Long, bright green, spiky needles curve away from twig. Round, spiky, green cones ripening to brown. Red-brown, peeling bark. Tall, narrow, cone-shaped tree.

▲ Juniper

Sharp, blue-green needles in threes with white band on upper surface. Berry-like cones turning purplish-black in second year. Often a shrub.

▲ Yew

Broad needles, dark green above and yellowish-green below, parted on twig. Red, berry-like fruits. Orange-brown flaking bark. Short stout trunk. Can be a hedge.

▲ Dawn Redwood

Soft, light green needles, similar to Swamp Cypress but larger, drop in winter. Young bark is orange and flaking, furrowed in older trees.

Needles parted on either side of twig

▲ Coast Redwood

Hard, sharp-pointed needles, dark green above and white-banded below. Small, round cones. Thick, reddish, spongy bark. Tall tree.

Foliage hanging from upswept branches

Diamond-shaped cone scales wrinkle when they ripen

▲ Wellingtonia

Deep green, scale-like, pointed leaves. Long-stalked, round, corky cones. Soft, thick, deeply-furrowed bark. Tall tree with upswept branches.

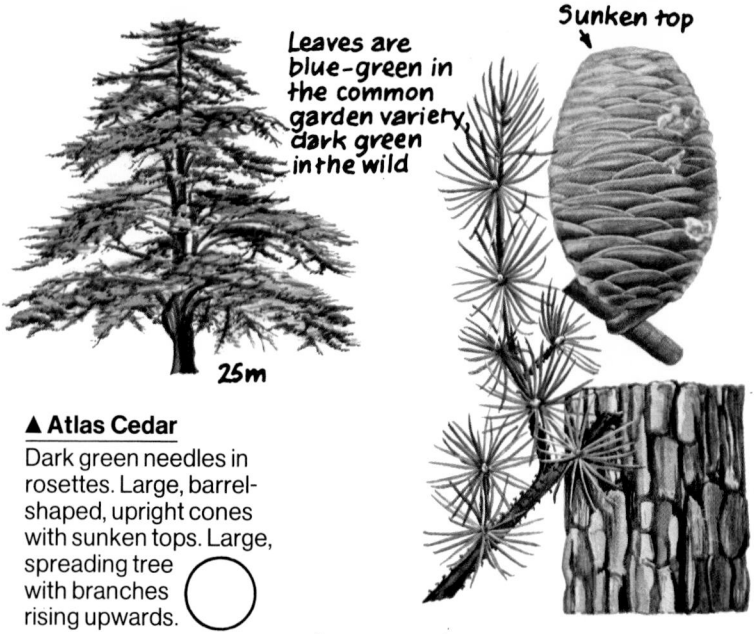

▲ Atlas Cedar

Dark green needles in rosettes. Large, barrel-shaped, upright cones with sunken tops. Large, spreading tree with branches rising upwards.

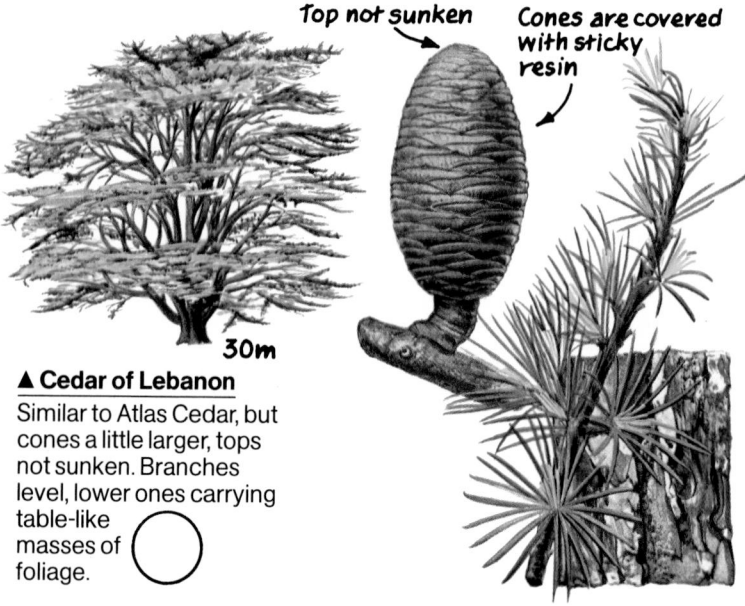

▲ Cedar of Lebanon

Similar to Atlas Cedar, but cones a little larger, tops not sunken. Branches level, lower ones carrying table-like masses of foliage.

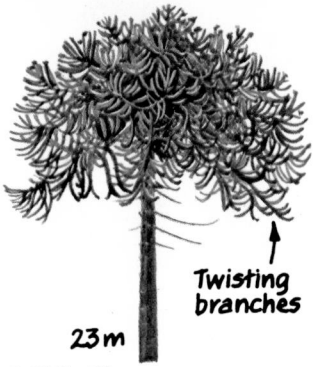

▲ Chile Pine

Also called Monkey Puzzle. Stiff, leathery, triangular leaves with sharp points, growing all round the shoot. Broad round crown. Pole-like trunk with wrinkled bark.

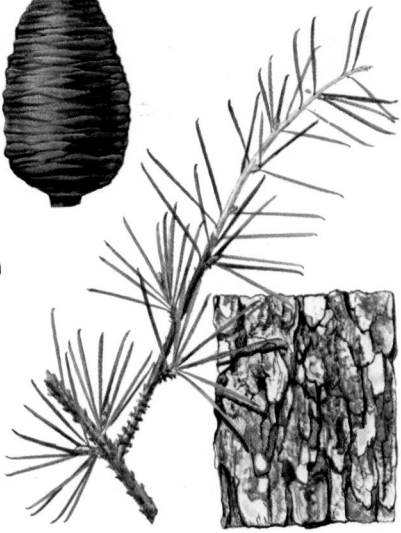

▲ Deodar

Leaves like other Cedars, but longer, softer, and paler green. Large, barrel-shaped cones have sunken top. Tall tree with pointed crown.

Broadleaved Trees

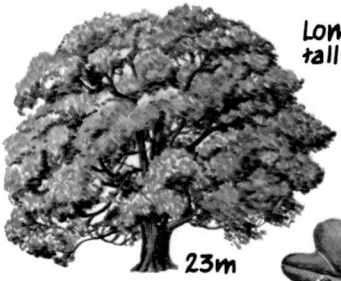

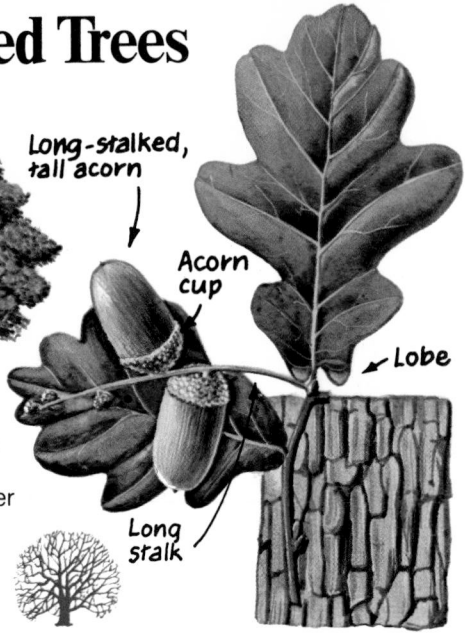

▲ English Oak

Leaves short-stalked with ear-like lobes at base. Broad crown. Trunk shorter than Sessile Oak. Many large branches growing from same point.

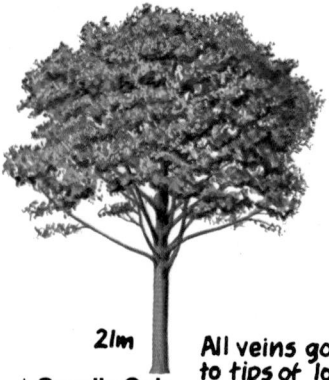

▲ Sessile Oak

Thick, dark green, long-stalked leaves tapering to base. Branches grow from stem at different levels and point upwards in narrow crown.

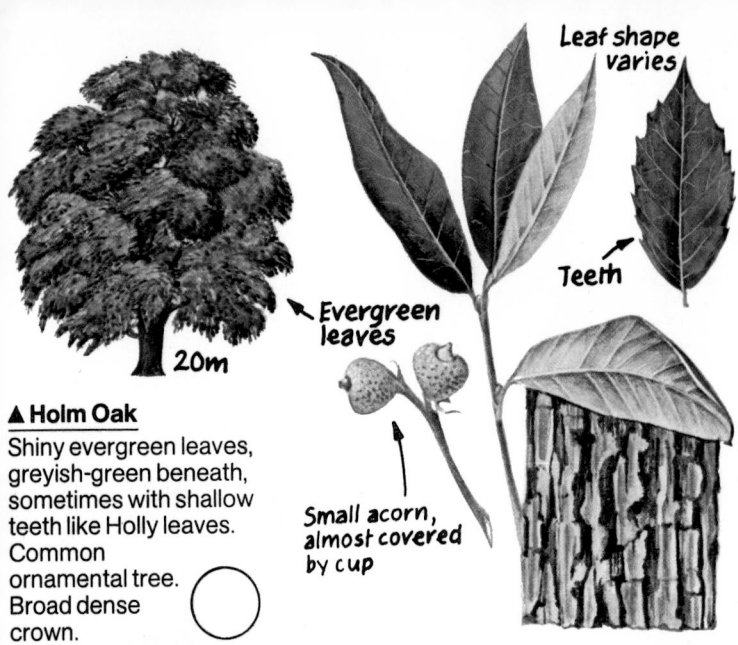

▲ Holm Oak

Shiny evergreen leaves, greyish-green beneath, sometimes with shallow teeth like Holly leaves. Common ornamental tree. Broad dense crown.

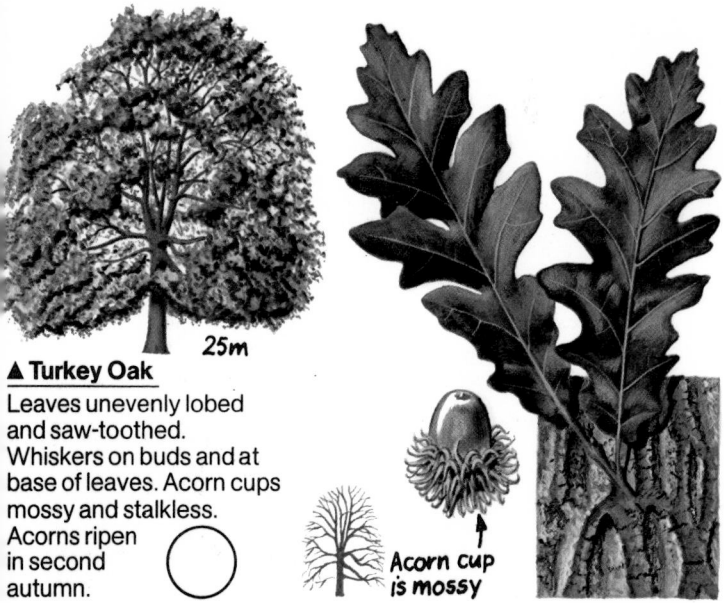

▲ Turkey Oak

Leaves unevenly lobed and saw-toothed. Whiskers on buds and at base of leaves. Acorn cups mossy and stalkless. Acorns ripen in second autumn.

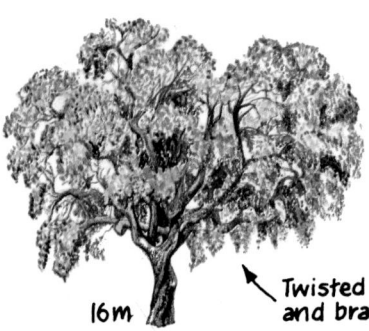

▲ Cork Oak

Shiny evergreen leaves with wavy edge. Thick, corky, whitish bark. Small tree, except in warmer countries. Common in southern Europe.

▲ Red Oak

Large leaves with bristly-tipped lobes, turn reddish-brown in autumn. Squat acorns in shallow cups ripen in second year. Smooth silvery bark.

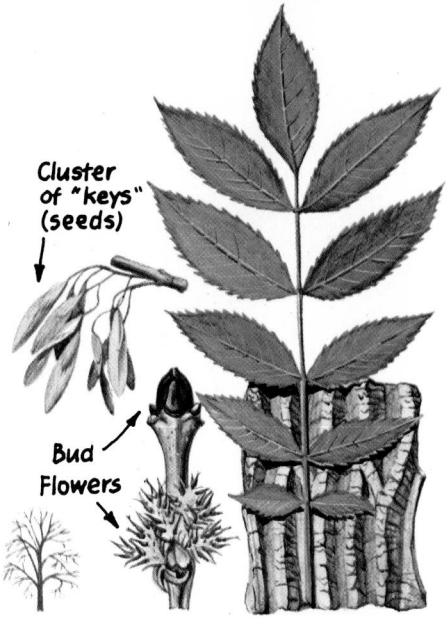

▲ Common Ash

Compound leaf of 9-13 leaflets appearing late, after bunches of purplish flowers. Clusters of "keys" stay on the tree into winter. Pale grey bark.

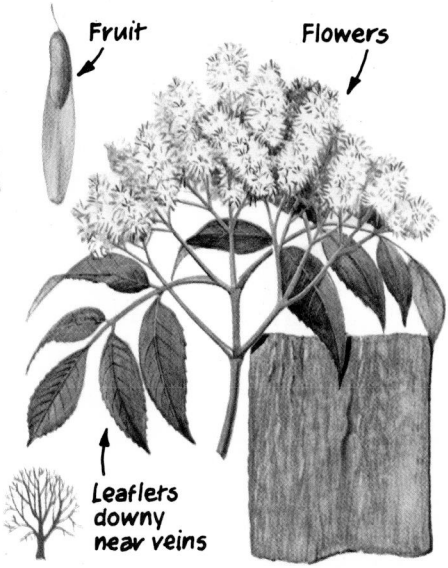

▲ Manna Ash

Compound leaf of 5-9 stalked leaflets. Clusters of showy white flowers in May. Smooth grey bark oozes sugary liquid called manna.

▲ Common Alder

Leaves rounded, falling in late autumn. Young twigs and leaves sticky. Reddish catkins. Fruits like small, brown, woody cones. Always near water.

▲ Grey Alder

Pointed oval leaves with sharply-toothed edge, soft and grey underneath. Twigs and bark grey. Catkins and fruit like Common Alder.

▲ Rowan

Compound leaf like Ash, but smaller. Clusters of creamy-white flowers in May. Red berries ripen in August. Small tree. Often grows alone on mountainsides.

▲ Whitebeam

Large oval leaves with toothed edge, white and furry underneath. Flowers and fruit like Rowan but ripen later. Grows at edges of woods.

▲ Aspen

Rounded leaves with wavy edge, trembling in wind. White downy catkins. Grey bark with large pores. Smaller than other Poplars. Often in thickets.

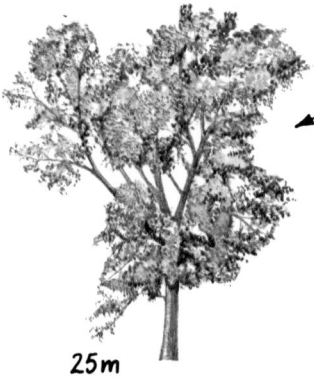

▲ Black Italian Poplar

Dark green, triangular, pointed leaves, appearing late. Red catkins. Deeply furrowed bark. Trunk and crown often lean away from wind. Grows fast.

▲ White Poplar

Five-lobed leaves are downy white underneath. Entire crown looks white. Lower bark dark and rugged, upper bark pale grey. Crown often leaning.

▲ Western Balsam Poplar

Large, triangular, pointed leaves, white underneath. Buds and young leaves sticky and sweet-smelling. Long purplish catkins. White fluffy seeds.

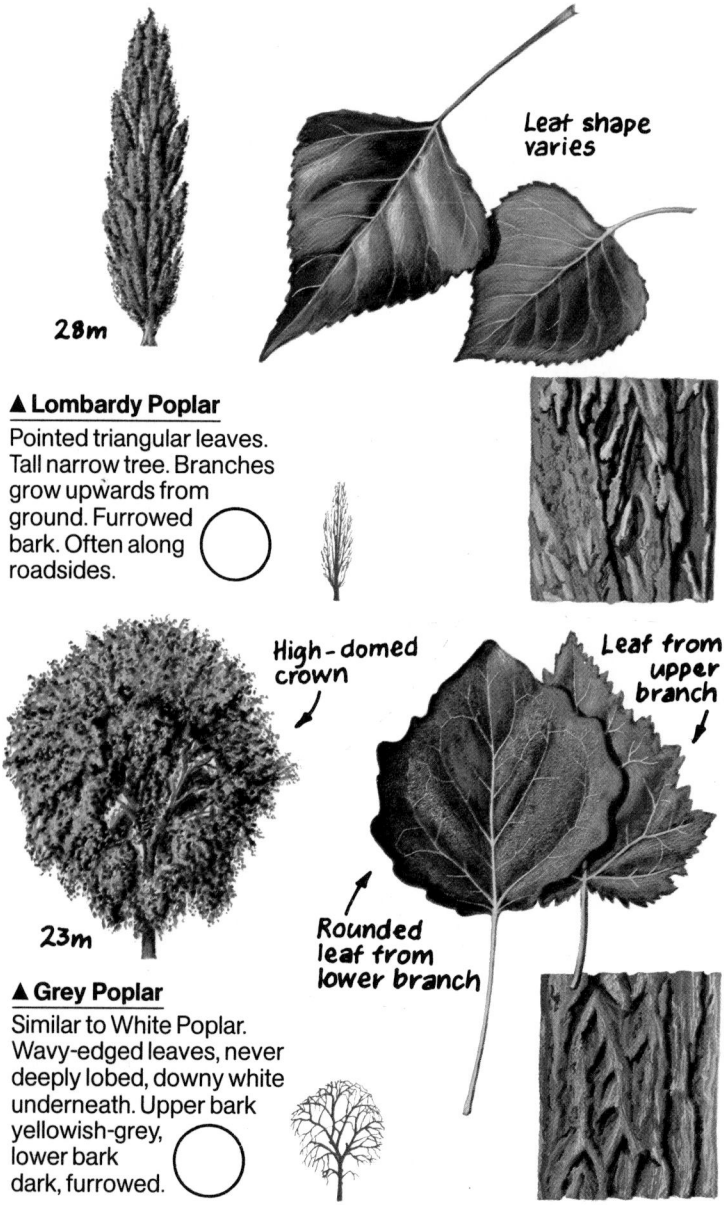

▲ Lombardy Poplar

Pointed triangular leaves. Tall narrow tree. Branches grow upwards from ground. Furrowed bark. Often along roadsides.

▲ Grey Poplar

Similar to White Poplar. Wavy-edged leaves, never deeply lobed, downy white underneath. Upper bark yellowish-grey, lower bark dark, furrowed.

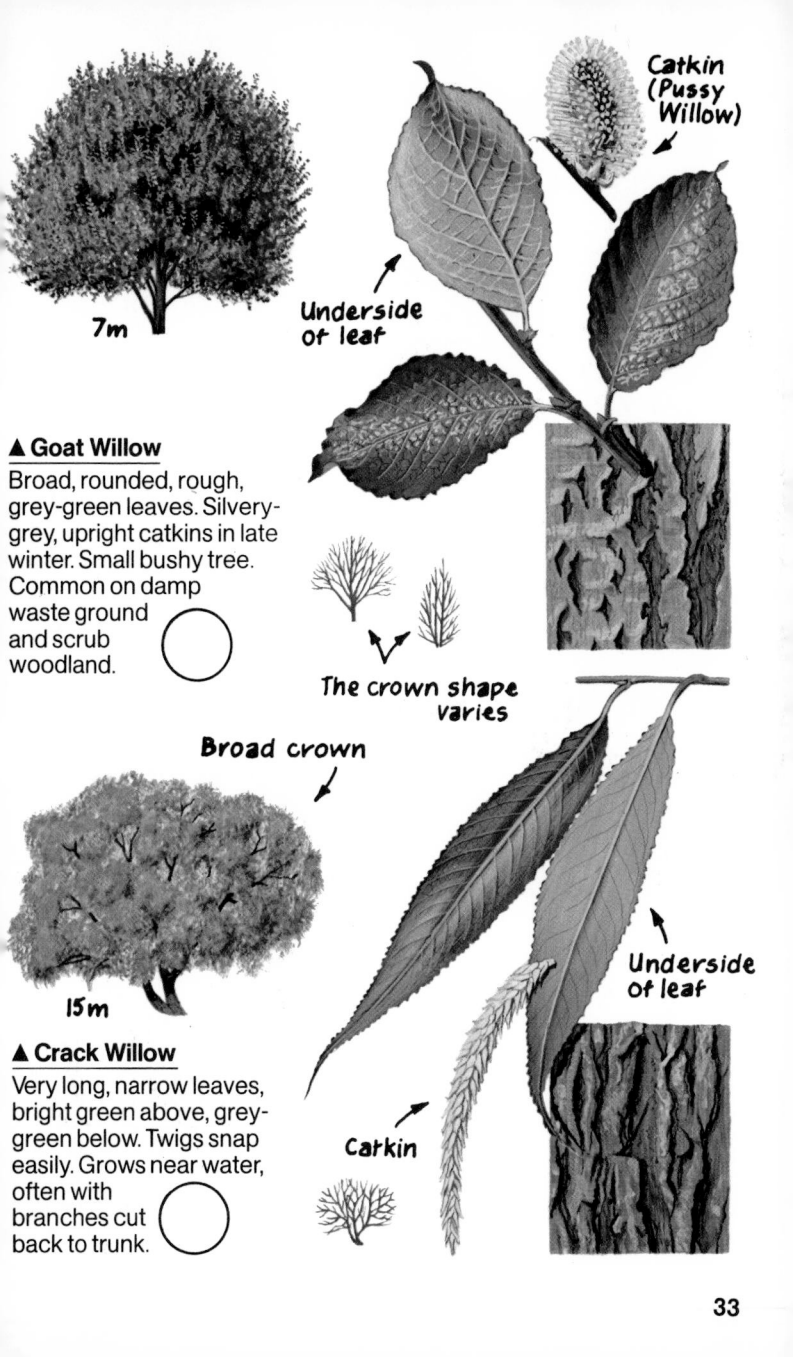

▲ Goat Willow

Broad, rounded, rough, grey-green leaves. Silvery-grey, upright catkins in late winter. Small bushy tree. Common on damp waste ground and scrub woodland.

▲ Crack Willow

Very long, narrow leaves, bright green above, grey-green below. Twigs snap easily. Grows near water, often with branches cut back to trunk.

▲ White Willow

Long, narrow, finely-toothed leaves, white underneath. Slender twigs, hard to break. Common by water. Weeping Willow is a variety with trailing branches.

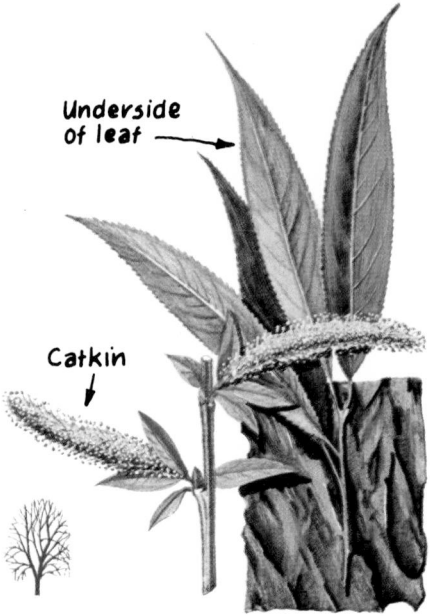

▲ Silver Birch

Small, diamond-shaped leaves with double-toothed edge. Long "lamb's tail" catkins in April. Slender tree with drooping branches.

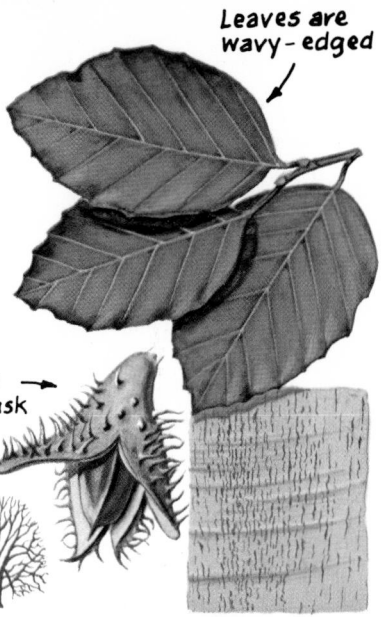

▲ Common Beech

Light green, oval leaves turn copper-brown in autumn. Triangular nuts in hairy husks. Tall tree with spreading crown. Smooth grey bark.

▲ Hornbeam

Sharply-toothed, oval leaves. In autumn, clusters of three-pronged, leaf-like wings hold nuts. Smooth grey bark is fluted (or rippled).

▲ Crab Apple

Small rounded leaves with toothed edge. Pinkish-white flowers in May. Small, speckled, reddish-green apples. Small bushy tree. Common in hedges.

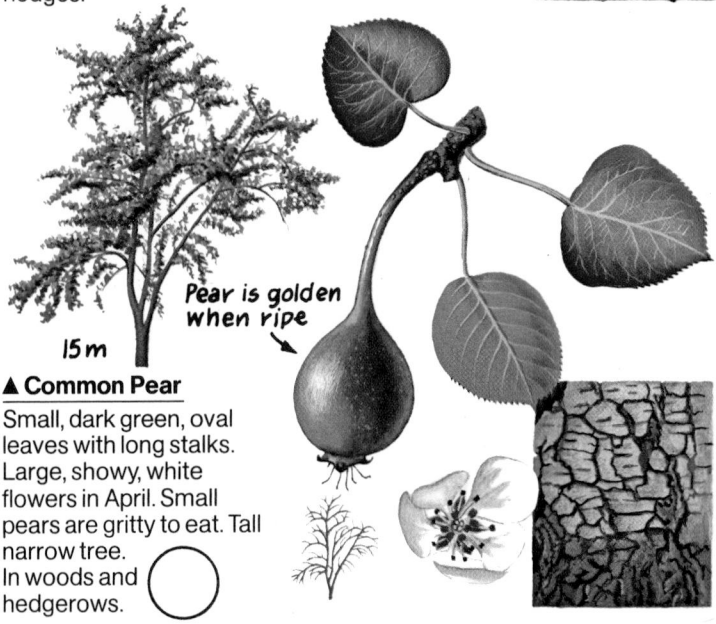

▲ Common Pear

Small, dark green, oval leaves with long stalks. Large, showy, white flowers in April. Small pears are gritty to eat. Tall narrow tree. In woods and hedgerows.

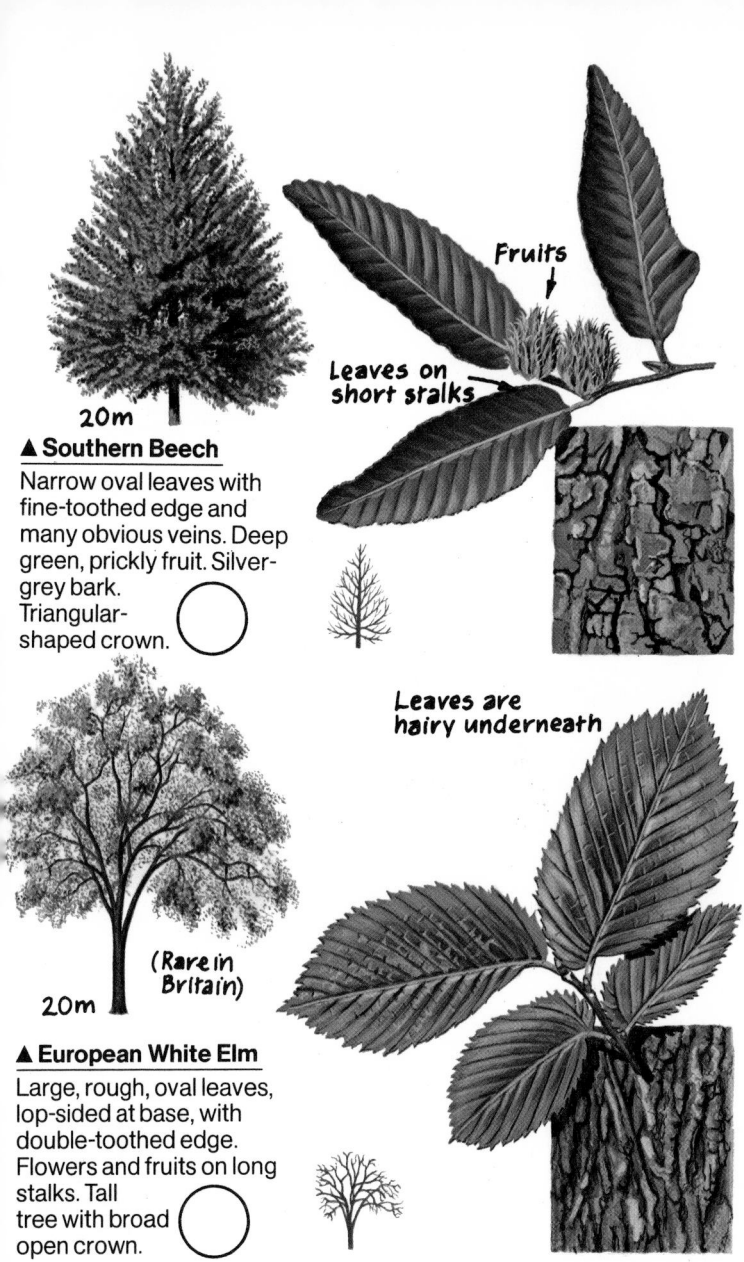

▲ Southern Beech

Narrow oval leaves with fine-toothed edge and many obvious veins. Deep green, prickly fruit. Silver-grey bark. Triangular-shaped crown.

▲ European White Elm

Large, rough, oval leaves, lop-sided at base, with double-toothed edge. Flowers and fruits on long stalks. Tall tree with broad open crown.

▲ London Plane

Large broad leaves with pointed lobes. Spiny "bobble" fruits hanging all winter. Flaking bark leaving yellowish patches. Tall tree, often in towns.

▲ Sycamore

Dark green, leathery leaves with five lobes. Paired, closely-angled, winged seeds. Large spreading tree. Smooth brown bark becoming scaly.

▲ Norway Maple

Light green, thin leaves. Lobes and teeth are bristle-tipped. Paired seeds form wide angle. Smaller, less spreading than Sycamore. Finely-furrowed, grey bark.

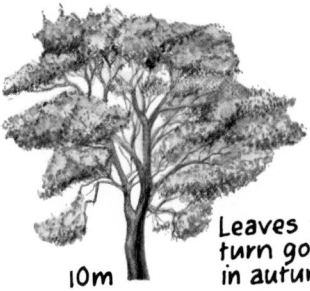

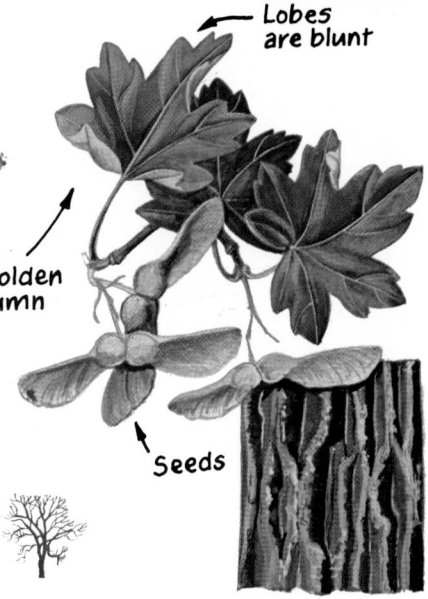

▲ Field Maple

Small, dark green leaves with five lobes. Small, reddish, winged seeds form a straight line. Small tree with round head. Often in hedges.

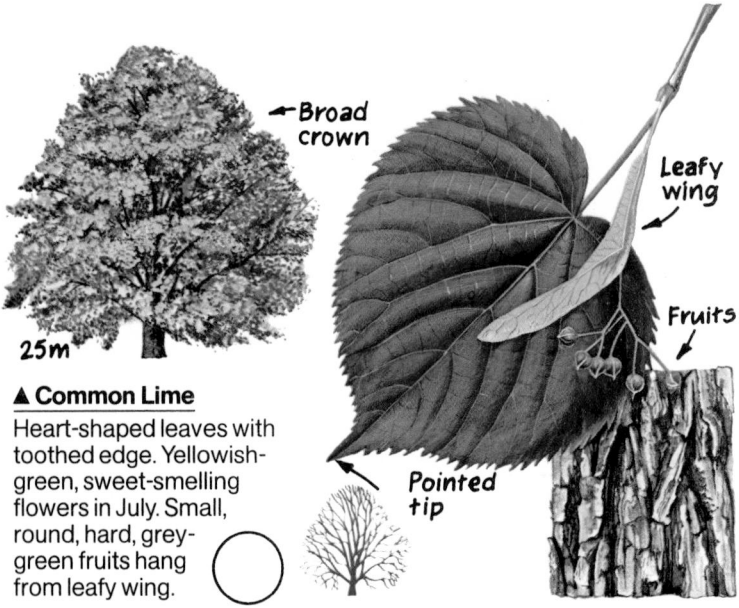

▲ Common Lime

Heart-shaped leaves with toothed edge. Yellowish-green, sweet-smelling flowers in July. Small, round, hard, grey-green fruits hang from leafy wing.

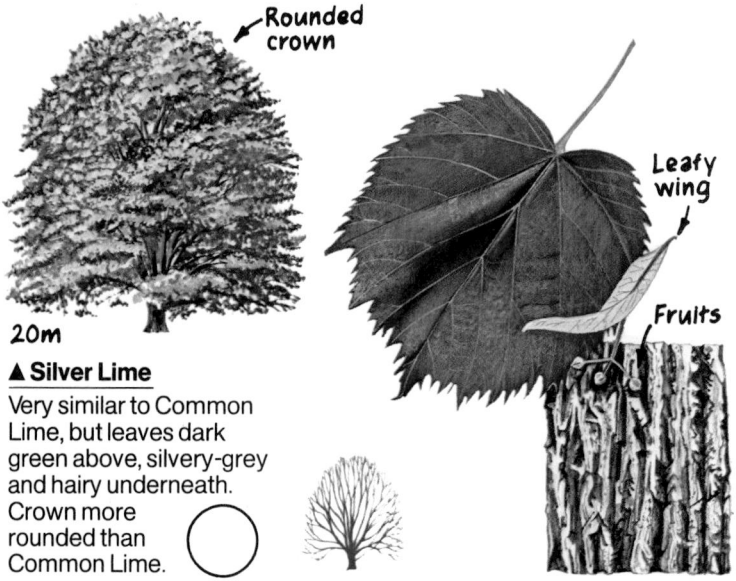

▲ Silver Lime

Very similar to Common Lime, but leaves dark green above, silvery-grey and hairy underneath. Crown more rounded than Common Lime.

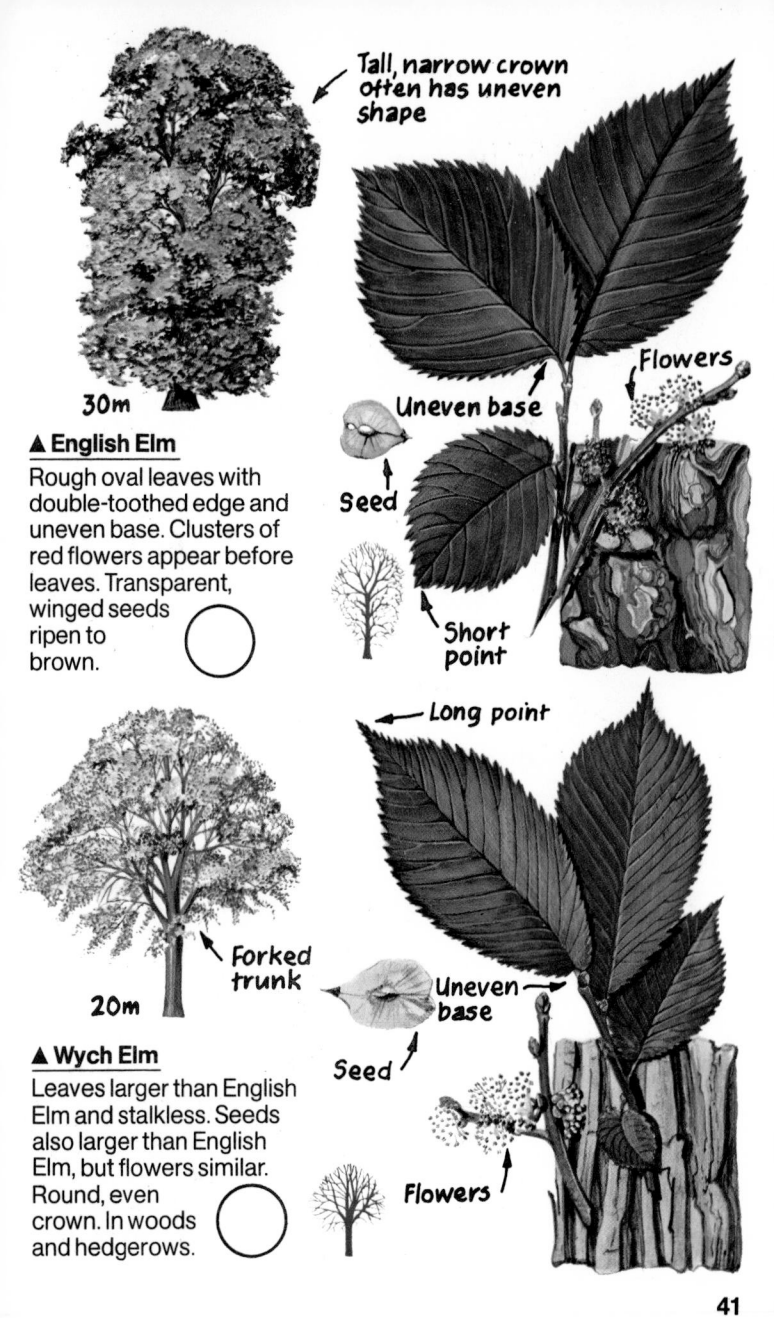

▲ English Elm

Rough oval leaves with double-toothed edge and uneven base. Clusters of red flowers appear before leaves. Transparent, winged seeds ripen to brown.

▲ Wych Elm

Leaves larger than English Elm and stalkless. Seeds also larger than English Elm, but flowers similar. Round, even crown. In woods and hedgerows.

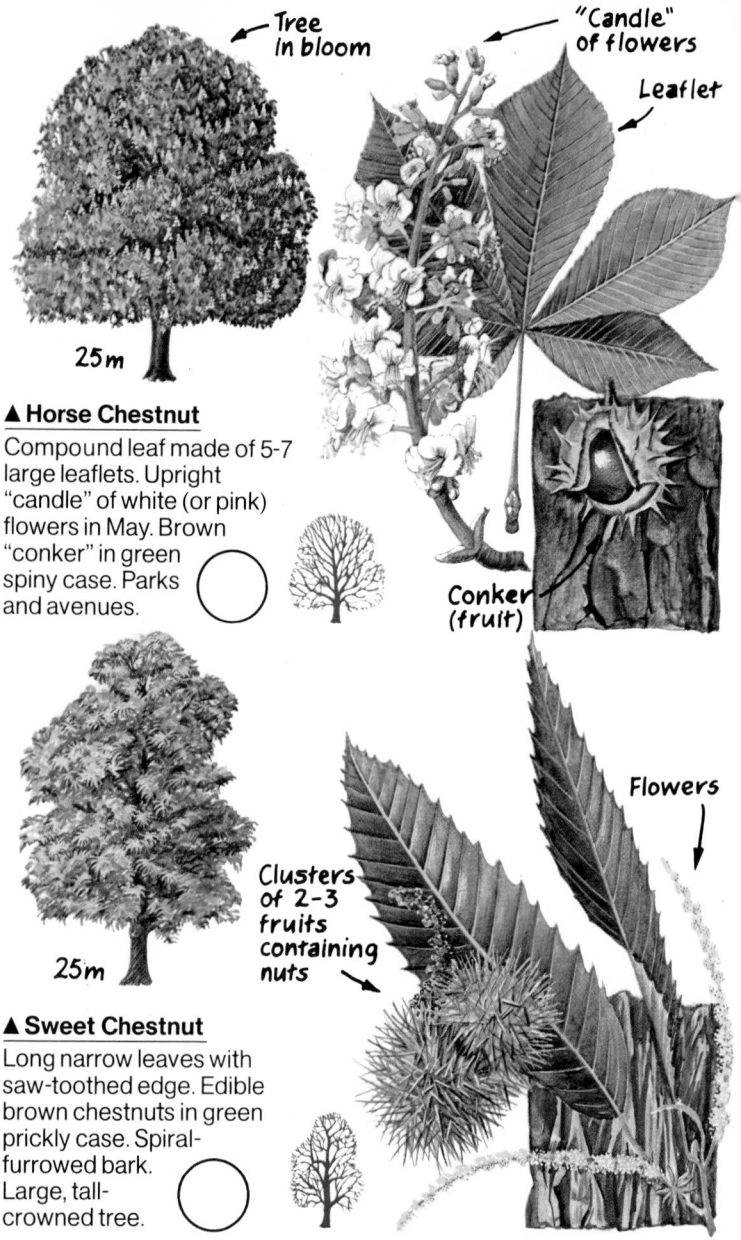

▲ Horse Chestnut

Compound leaf made of 5-7 large leaflets. Upright "candle" of white (or pink) flowers in May. Brown "conker" in green spiny case. Parks and avenues.

▲ Sweet Chestnut

Long narrow leaves with saw-toothed edge. Edible brown chestnuts in green prickly case. Spiral-furrowed bark. Large, tall-crowned tree.

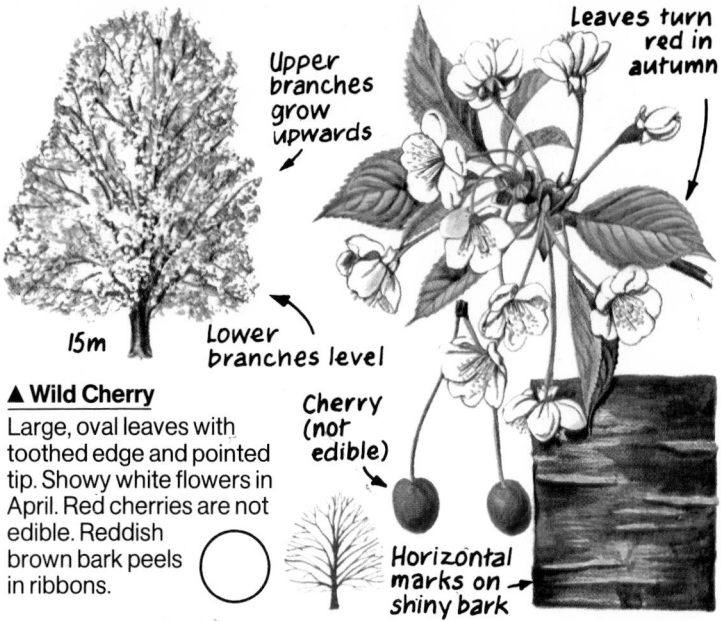

▲ Wild Cherry

Large, oval leaves with toothed edge and pointed tip. Showy white flowers in April. Red cherries are not edible. Reddish brown bark peels in ribbons.

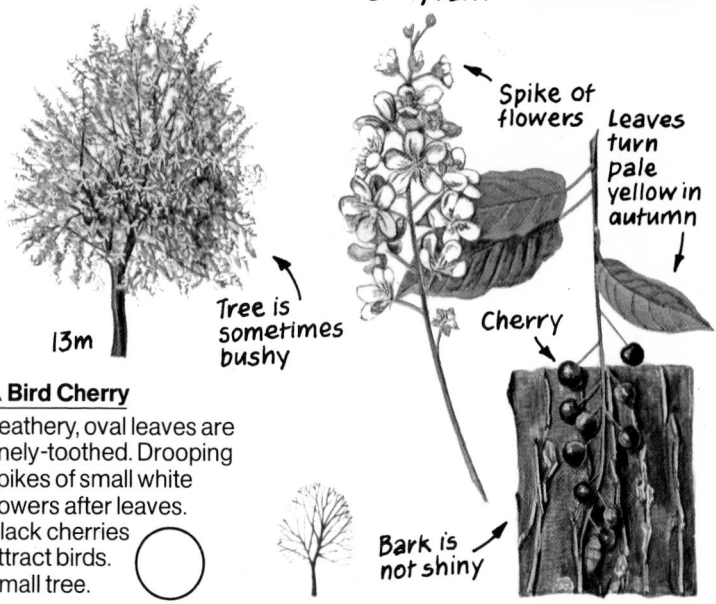

▲ Bird Cherry

Leathery, oval leaves are finely-toothed. Drooping spikes of small white flowers after leaves. Black cherries attract birds. Small tree.

▲ Black Mulberry

Rough, heart-shaped leaves with toothed edge. Short catkins. Edible, blackish-red berries. Low, broad-crowned tree. Short trunk and twisted branches.

▲ Common Walnut

Compound leaves of 7-9 untoothed leaflets. Twigs are hollow, with cross-sections inside. Smooth grey bark with some cracks, or fissures. Broad crown.

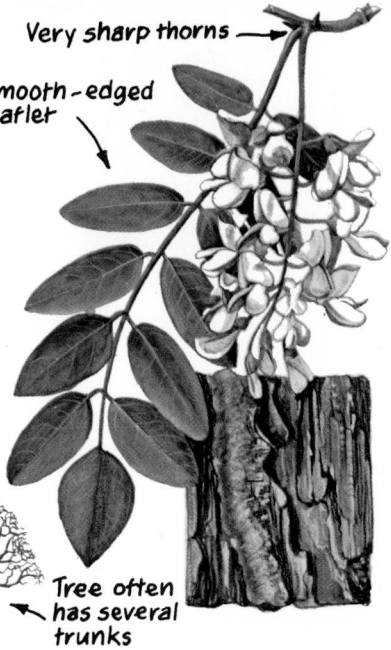

▲ False Acacia

Compound leaves of many small leaflets. Pairs of sharp thorns on twigs. Hanging clusters of white flowers in June. Seeds in pods. Deeply-furrowed bark.

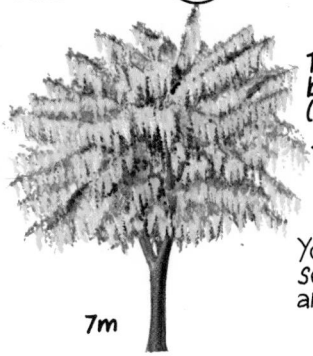

▲ Laburnum

Leaf made up of three leaflets. Hanging clusters of yellow flowers. Poisonous seeds in twisted brown pods. Small tree. Smooth, green-brown bark.

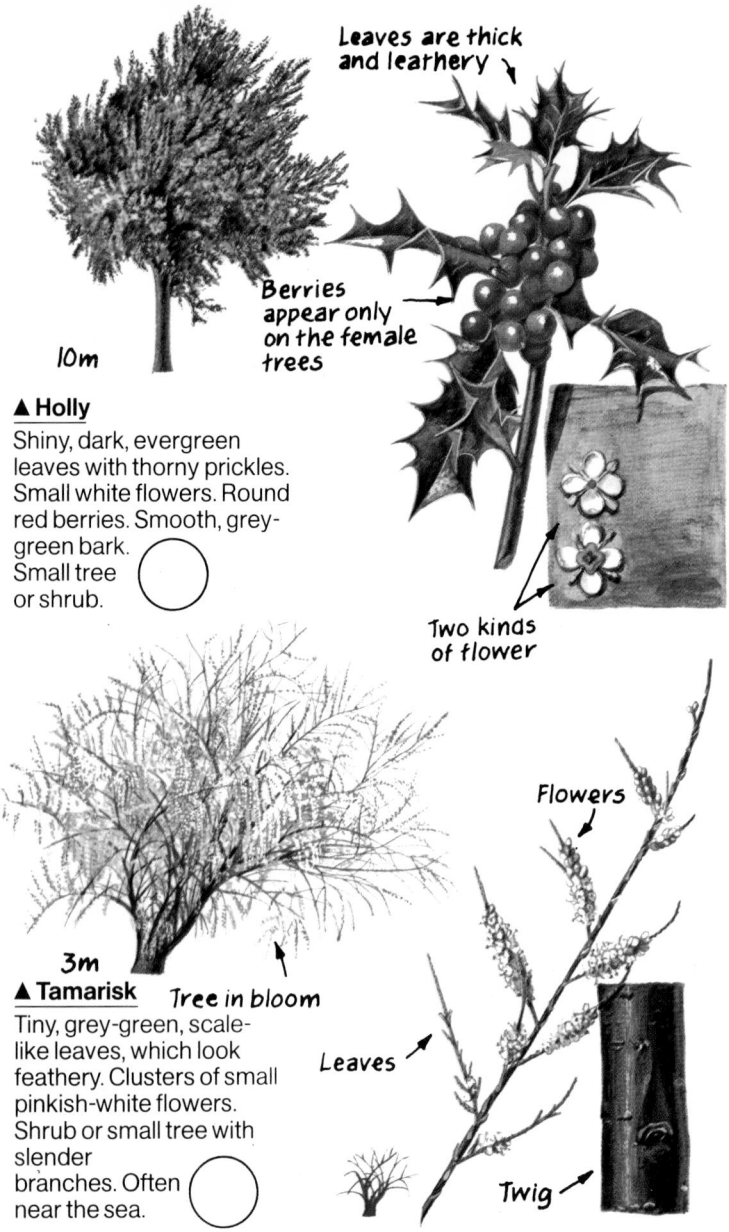

▲ Holly

Shiny, dark, evergreen leaves with thorny prickles. Small white flowers. Round red berries. Smooth, grey-green bark. Small tree or shrub.

▲ Tamarisk

Tiny, grey-green, scale-like leaves, which look feathery. Clusters of small pinkish-white flowers. Shrub or small tree with slender branches. Often near the sea.

▲ Common Olive

Narrow evergreen leaves in pairs. Clusters of small whitish flowers. Fleshy green fruit ripens to black. Small tree with twisted trunk.

▲ European Fan Palm

Large, fan-shaped leaves made up of 12-15 stiff, pointed parts. Large clusters of small flowers and fruits. Wild plants form trunkless clumps of leaves.

▲ Tulip Tree

Smooth, four-lobed leaves, golden in autumn. Large tulip-like flowers in June. Upright, brown, cone-like fruits. Tall, narrow-crowned tree.

▲ Maidenhair Tree

Double-lobed, fan shaped leaves with deep cleft, bright yellow in autumn. Hanging fruit on female trees. Male trees more common. Tall slender tree.

Shrubs

▲ Sea Buckthorn

Long, narrow, greyish-green leaves. Thorny twigs. Tiny, green flowers. Orange berries. Grows in dense thickets mainly by the sea.

▲ Alder Buckthorn

Dull green, oval leaves, turning yellow in autumn. Small greenish flowers. Red berries turn black when ripe. Small tree or shrub. Damp places.

▲ Common Hawthorn

Shiny, dark green leaves, deeply-lobed. Clusters of small white flowers in May. Dark red berries. Twigs thorny. Rounded crown. Thickets and hedgerows.

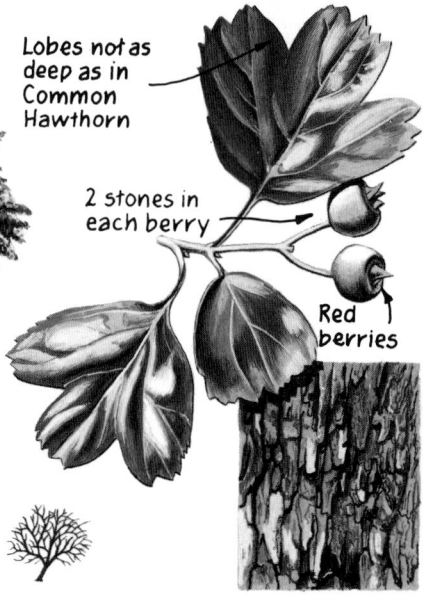

▲ Midland Hawthorn

Similar to Common Hawthorn, but leaves rounded with shallow lobes. Flowers usually white, but red-flowered variety common in parks and gardens.

▲ Guelder Rose

Leaves with 3-5 toothed lobes, turning russet in autumn. Clusters of white flowers, inner flowers much smaller. Red berries. Hedgerow shrub.

▲ Wild Service Tree

Leaves five-lobed, turning deep red in autumn. Clusters of white flowers in May. Drab brown, speckled berries. Small rounded tree.

Identifying Winter Buds

In winter you can identify broad-leaved trees by their winter buds.

English Oak
Clusters of stout, light brown buds on rugged twigs.

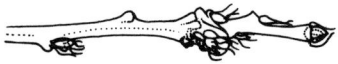

Turkey Oak
Clusters of small, brown, whiskered buds.

Red Oak
Clusters of reddish-brown buds on grey-green twigs with large bud at the tip.

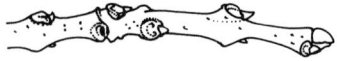

Ash
Large black buds on silver-grey twigs.

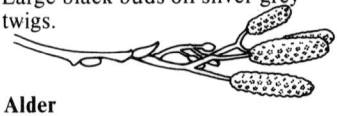

Alder
Stalked violet buds. Male catkins often present.

Rowan
Large blackish end bud with tuft of white hairs.

White Poplar
Small, orange-brown bud covered by white felty hairs on green twigs.

White Willow
Slender buds enclosed in a single scale, close to pinkish downy twig.

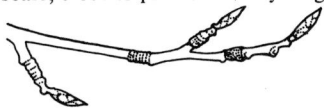

Common Beech
Long pointed, copper-brown buds sticking out from brown twigs.

Hornbeam
Dull brown or green buds, close to fine, greyish-brown twigs.

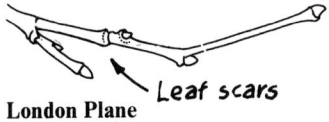

London Plane
Brown, cone-shaped buds with ring scars round them.

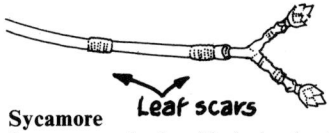

Sycamore
Large green buds with dark-edged scales on stout, light brown twigs.

English Elm
Pointed, hairy, chocolate-brown buds on stout twigs.

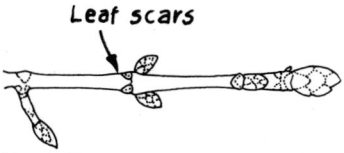

Horse Chestnut
Large, sticky, brown buds on stout twigs, with obvious leaf scars.

Sweet Chestnut
Rounded, reddish-brown buds on knobbly, greenish-brown twigs.

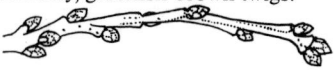

Wild Cherry
Fat, shiny, red-brown buds grouped at tip of light brown twigs.

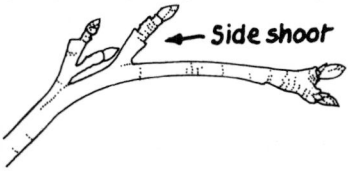

Crab Apple
Small, hairy, brown, triangle-shaped buds, often bent to one side, on shiny twigs.

Common Walnut
Big, black, velvety, triangle-shaped buds on stout, hollow twigs.

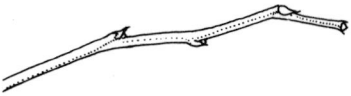

False Acacia
Small buds with thorns at base on grey, crooked, ribbed twigs.

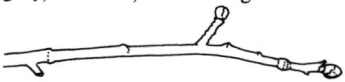

Wild Service Tree
Flat, green buds with brown-edged scales on thick, light-brown twigs.

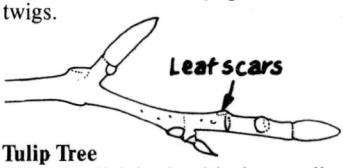

Tulip Tree
Flat, purplish buds with short stalk on light brown twigs.

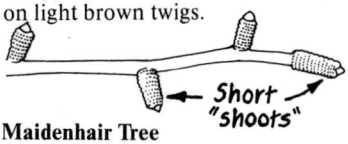

Maidenhair Tree
Squat, reddish-brown buds on fawn-coloured twigs.

Common Lime
Reddish-brown, lop-sided buds on reddish twigs.

Bark Quiz

Name the trees these bark rubbings are from. The answers are upside-down at the bottom of the page.

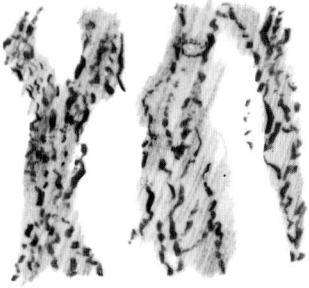

1 _____

2 _____

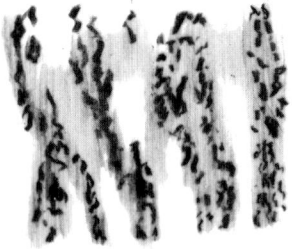

3 _____

4 _____

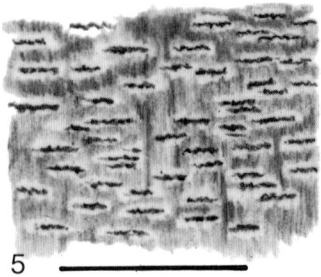

5 _____

6 _____

1. Walnut 2. London Plane 3. English Oak 4. Common Beech 5. Silver Birch 6. Sweet Chestnut 7. Scots Pine 8. Whitebeam 9. Lombardy Poplar 10. Larch.

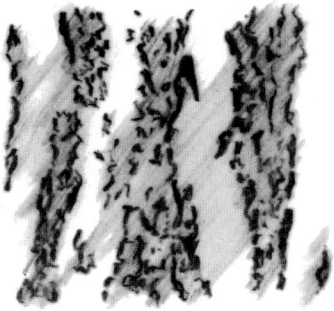

7 _____

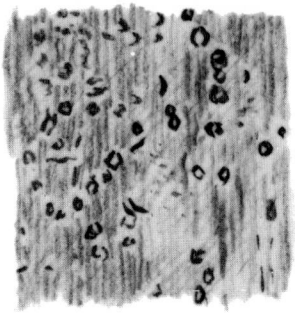

8 _____

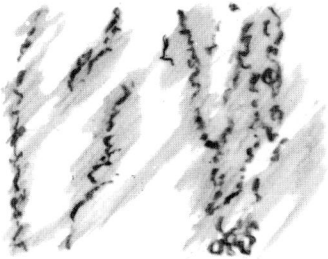

9 _____

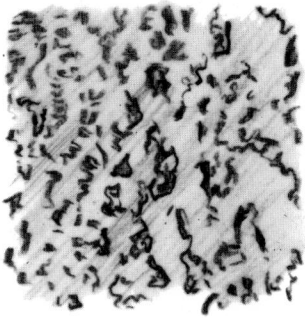

10 _____

Making Bark Rubbings

To make bark rubbings, you need strong thin paper, wax crayons and sellotape. Tape a piece of paper against the trunk of a tree. Rub firmly up and down on the paper with the crayon until the bark pattern appears. Be careful not to tear the paper when rubbing.

Match the Fruits to the Trees

Match the numbered fruits to the trees on which they grow. The answers are upside-down at the bottom of the opposite page.

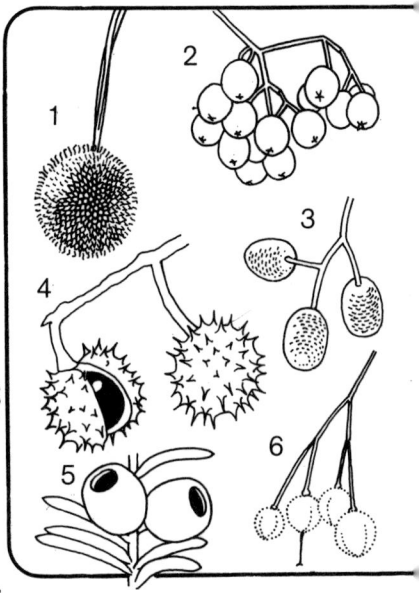

1. London Plane 2. Rowan 3. Alder 4. Horse Chestnut 5. Yew 6. Lime 7. Crab Apple
8. Bird Cherry 9. Olive 10. Tulip Tree 11. Black Mulberry 12. Holly

Growing Seedlings

Try growing your own tree from a seed. Pick ripe seeds from trees or from the ground. Acorns are especially easy to find and grow, but almost any fresh seed will do. Most seeds take a couple of months to sprout.

1

Soak the acorns or other hard nuts overnight in warm water. Take the cups off the acorns, but do not try to remove their shells.

2

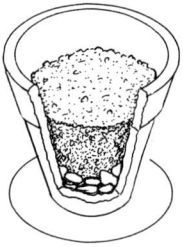

Put some stones or pebbles in the bottom of a flower pot. This will help the water to drain properly. Fill the pot with soil or compost until the pot is almost full. Place a saucer under the pot and water the soil well.

3

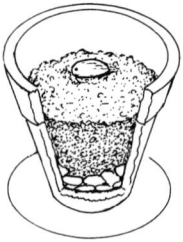

Because the seeds need plenty of room to grow, place only one seed in each pot that you have prepared. Cover the seed with a thin layer of soil. Press the soil down to make it firm. Water the soil again lightly.

4

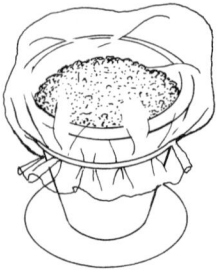

Place a plastic bag over the top of each pot and fasten it with string or a rubber band. This will help to keep the soil inside the pot moist without any watering. Place the pot on a window-sill if possible, or in a sunny place. Wait for the seeds to sprout.

5

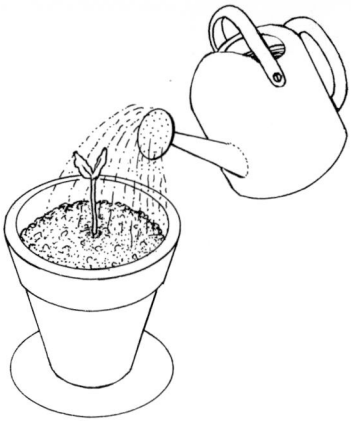

Remove the plastic bags from the pots as soon as you can see the seedlings growing. Water the seedlings twice a week. The soil should be damp, but not too wet or else the seedlings may rot.

Seedling leaves often look different from the tree's later leaves.

6

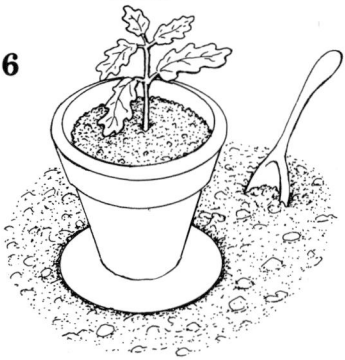

If you can, place your seedlings outside in the summer. In autumn, you can transplant the seedlings into the ground. However, if your prefer, you can leave them in pots indoors throughout the winter.

7

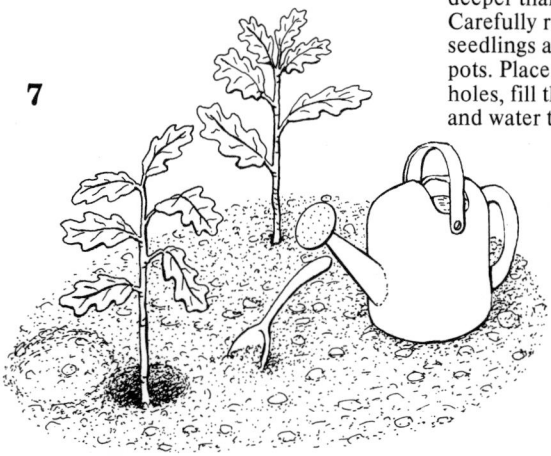

Dig holes which are a bit deeper than the pots. Carefully remove the seedlings and soil from the pots. Place them in the holes, fill them in with soil and water them often.

Books to Read

For identification: *Know Your Broadleaves* and *Know Your Conifers*. H. L. Edlin (H.M.S.O.). Two paperbacks from the Forestry Commission. Good value.
Trees in Britain. (Jarrold). A series of five cheap booklets, with colour photographs.
A Field Guide to the Trees of Britain and Northern Europe. A. Mitchell (Collins). Good, detailed reference book to carry round.
Trees of the world. S. Leathart (Hamlyn).
Large book with colour photographs.Worth getting out of the library.
Trees and Bushes of Europe. O. Polunin (Oxford).
Lots of colour photographs.
For reading: *The NatureTrail Book of Trees & Leaves*. I. Selberg (Usborne). Facts about trees and how they grow. Lots of projects, eg. making a tree survey and making leaf tiles. Good value.
The World of a Tree. A. Darlington (Faber). All about the animals and insects that live in and around trees.
Town & Country: Growing Trees. I. Finch (Longman). How trees grow. Cheap paperback.

Places to Visit

These are gardens open to the public and are very good places to spot trees.
Royal Botanic Gardens, Kew, Richmond, Surrey.
Regent's Park, London.
Hyde Park, London.
Royal Horticultural Society Gardens, Wisley, Ripley, Surrey.
Borde Hill, Haywards Heath, Sussex.
Royal Botanic Gardens, Wakehurst Place, Ardingly, nr. Haywards Heath, Sussex.
Sheffield Park, Uckfield, Sussex.
Winkworth Arboretum, Godalming, Surrey.
Syon House, Brentford, Middx.
Cambridge University Botanic Gardens, Cambridge.
Oxford University Botanic Gardens, Oxford.
The National Pinetum, Bedgebury, Goudhurst, Kent.
Savill Gardens, Windsor, Berks.
Bolderwood Arboretum, New Forest, Hants.
Exebury, Beaulieu, Hants.
Eastnor Castle, Ledbury, Herefordshire.
Stourhead, Mere, Wilts.
Westonbirt Arboretum, nr. Tetbury, Glos.
Speech House, Coleford, Glos.
Bath Botanic Gardens, Bath, Avon.
Bicton Gardens, East Budleigh, Devon.
Liverpool University Botanic Gardens, Liverpool.
Chatsworth House, Derbyshire.
Harlow Car Gardens, Harrogate, Yorks.
Bodnant Gardens, Tal-y-cefn, Conway, Clwyd.
Vivod Forest Garden, Llangollen, Clwyd.
Royal Botanic Gardens, Edinburgh.
Inverary Castle, Argyllshire.
Younger Botanic Gardens, Benmore, by Dunoon, Argyllshire.
Diana's Grove, Blair Castle, Blair Atholl, Perthshire.

Latin Names

Here is a list of the names of the trees in this book, in Latin. The common (English) name may vary from one part of the country to another, but the Latin name remains the same.

p. 6 Pinus silvestris
Pinus pinaster
p. 7 Pinus pinea
Pinus contorta var. contorta
p. 8 Pinus nigra var. maritima
Pinus halepensis
p. 9 Pinus cembra
Pinus radiata
p. 10 Picea abies
Picea sitchensis
p. 11 Larix decidua
Larix kaempferi
p. 12 Chamaecyparis nootkatensis
Abies alba
p. 13 Abies cephalonica
Abies pinsapo
p. 14 Abies grandis
Abies procera
p. 15 Pseudotsuga menziesii
Tsuga heterophylla
p. 16 Thuja plicata
Chamaecyparis lawsoniana
p. 17 Cupressus sempervirens
Cupressus macrocarpa
p. 18 Taxodium distichum
Cupressocyparis leylandii
p. 19 Cryptomeria japonica
Juniperus communis
p. 20 Taxus baccata
Metasequoia glyptostroboides
p. 21 Sequoia sempervirens
Sequoiadendron giganteum
p. 22 Cedrus atlantica
Cedrus libani
p. 23 Araucaria araucana
Cedrus deodara
p. 24 Quercus robur
Quercus petraea
p. 25 Quercus ilex
Quercus cerris
p. 26 Quercus suber
Quercus borealis
p. 27 Fraxinus excelsior
Fraxinus ornus
p. 28 Alnus glutinosa
Alnus incana
p. 29 Sorbus aucuparia
Sorbus aria
p. 30 Populus tremula
Populus serotina
p. 31 Populus alba
Populus trichocarpa
p. 32 Populus nigra 'Italica'
Populus canescens
p. 33 Salix caprea
Salix fragilis
p. 34 Salix alba
Betula pendula
p. 35 Fagus silvatica
Carpinus betulus
p. 36 Malus silvestris
Pyrus communis
p. 37 Nothofagus procera
Ulmus laevis
p. 38 Platanus hispanica
Acer pseudoplatanus
p. 39 Acer platanoides
Acer campestre
p. 40 Tilia europaea
Tilia tomentosa
p. 41 Ulmus procera
Ulmus glabra
p. 42 Aesculus hippocastanum
Castanea sativa
p. 43 Prunus avium
Prunus padus
p. 44 Morus nigra
Juglans regia
p. 45 Robinia pseudoacacia
Laburnum anagyroides
p. 46 Ilex aquifolium
Tamarix gallica
p. 47 Olea europea
Chamaerops humilis
p. 48 Liriodendron tulipifera
Ginkgo biloba
p. 49 Hippophae rhamnoides
Frangula alnus
p. 50 Crataegus monogyna
Crataegus laevigata
p. 51 Viburnum opulus
Sorbus torminalis

Index

Acacia, False, 45, 53
Alder, Common, 28, 52; Grey, 28
Apple, Crab, 36, 53
Ash, Common, 27, 52; Manna, 27
Aspen, 30

bark, 5
Beech, Common, 35, 52;
  Southern, 37
Birch, Silver, 34
bract, 5
Buckthorn, Alder, 49; Sea, 49

Cedar, Atlas, 22; Japanese Red, 19;
  of Lebanon, 22; Western Red, 16
Cherry, Bird, 43; Wild, 43, 53
Chestnut, Horse, 42, 53;
  Sweet, 42, 53
cones, 5
crown, 5
Cypress, Italian, 17; Lawson, 16;
  Leyland, 18; Monterey, 17;
  Nootka, 12; Swamp, 18

Deodar, 23

Elm, English, 41, 53; European
  White, 37; Wych, 41

Fir, Douglas, 15; European
  Silver, 12; Grand, 14; Greek, 13;
  Noble, 14; Spanish, 13
flowers, 5
fruits, 5

Guelder Rose, 51

Hawthorn, Common, 50; Midland,
  50
Hemlock, Western, 15
Holly, 46
Hornbeam, 35, 52

Juniper, 19

Laburnum, 45
Larch European, 11; Japanese, 11
leaves, 4
Lime, Common, 40, 53; Silver, 40

Maidenhair Tree, 48, 53
Maple, Field, 39; Norway, 39
Monkey Puzzle, *see* Pine, Chile
Mulberry, Black, 44

Oak, Cork, 26; English, 24, 52;
  Holm, 25; Red, 26, 52;
  Sessile, 24; Turkey, 25, 52
Olive, Common, 47

Palm, European Fan, 47
Pear, Common, 36
Pine, Aleppo, 8; Chile, 23;
  Corsican, 8; Maritime, 6;
  Monterey, 9; Scots, 6; Shore, 7;
  Stone, 7; Swiss Stone, 9
Plane, London, 38, 52
Poplar, Black Italian, 30; Grey, 32;
  Lombardy, 32; Western Balsam,
  31; White, 31, 52

Redwood, Coast, 21; Dawn, 20
Rowan, 29, 52

seeds, 5
Service Tree, Wild, 51, 53
Spruce, Norway, 10; Sitka, 10
Sycamore, 38, 52

Tamarisk, 46
Tulip Tree, 48, 53

Walnut, Common, 44, 53
Wellingtonia, 21
Whitebeam, 29
Willow, Crack, 33; Goat, 33;
  White, 34, 52

Yew, 20

Scorecard

The trees on this scorecard are arranged in the same order as they appear in the book. When you go spotting, fill in the date at the top of one of the blank columns, and then write in that column your score, next to each tree that you see. At the end of the day, add up your scores and put the total at the bottom of the columns.

Page	Tree	Score	Date	Date	Date
6	Scots Pine	5			
6	Maritime Pine	15			
7	Stone Pine	25			
7	Shore Pine	10			
8	Corsican Pine	10			
8	Aleppo Pine	25			
9	Monterey Pine	15			
9	Swiss Stone Pine	25			
10	Norway Spruce	5			
10	Sitka Spruce	10			
11	European Larch	5			
11	Japanese Larch	10			
12	European Silver Fir	10			
12	Nootka Cypress	15			
13	Greek Fir	20			
13	Spanish Fir	20			
14	Grand Fir	15			
14	Noble Fir	10			
15	Douglas Fir	5			
15	Western Hemlock	10			
	Total				

Page	Tree	Score			
16	Western Red Cedar	10			
16	Lawson Cypress	5			
17	Italian Cypress	20			
17	Monterey Cypress	15			
18	Leyland Cypress	15			
18	Swamp Cypress	15			
19	Japanese Red Cedar	15			
19	Juniper	15			
20	Yew	5			
20	Dawn Redwood	20			
21	Coast Redwood	15			
21	Wellingtonia	15			
22	Atlas Cedar	10			
22	Cedar of Lebanon	10			
23	Chile Pine	10			
23	Deodar	10			
24	English Oak	5			
24	Sessile Oak	5			
25	Holm Oak	10			
25	Turkey Oak	10			
	Total				

Page	Tree	Score			
26	Cork Oak	20			
26	Red Oak	10			
27	Common Ash	5			
27	Manna Ash	15			
28	Common Alder	5			
28	Grey Alder	15			
29	Rowan	5			
29	Whitebeam	10			
30	Aspen	15			
30	Black Ital. Poplar	10			
31	White Poplar	10			
31	Western Balsam Pop.	10			
32	Lombardy Poplar	10			
32	Grey Poplar	10			
33	Goat Willow	5			
33	Crack Willow	15			
34	White Willow	10			
34	Silver Birch	5			
35	Common Beech	5			
35	Hornbeam	10			
36	Crab Apple	10			
36	Common Pear	20			
37	Southern Beech	20			
		Total			

Page	Tree	Score			
37	European White Elm	25			
38	London Plane	10			
38	Sycamore	5			
39	Norway Maple	10			
39	Field Maple	15			
40	Common Lime	10			
40	Silver Lime	20			
41	English Elm	5			
41	Wych Elm	5			
42	Horse Chestnut	5			
42	Sweet Chestnut	5			
43	Wild Cherry	5			
43	Bird Cherry	10			
44	Black Mulberry	20			
44	Common Walnut	10			
45	False Acacia	10			
45	Laburnum	5			
46	Holly	5			
46	Tamarisk	15			
47	Common Olive	25			
47	European Fan Palm	15			
48	Tulip Tree	20			
48	Maidenhair Tree	20			
		Total			